2.25

The Bible says...

by Jack Cottrell

You may obtain a 64-page leader's guide to accompany this paperback. Order number 41015 from Standard Publishing or your local supplier.

A Division of Standard Publishing
Cincinnati, Ohio 45231

euthanasia · suicide · racism · human engineering
abortion · activism · authority · citizenship
drugs · war · government
capital punishment
justice

Unless otherwise noted, Scripture quotations are from the New American Standard Bible, © The Lockman Foundation 1971, and are used by permission.

© 1982, The STANDARD PUBLISHING CO., division of STANDEX INTERNATIONAL Corp.

Library of Congress Cataloging in Publication Data

Cottrell, Jack.
  The Bible says . . .

  Summary: Focuses on such topics as authority, citizenship, responsibility, war, abortion, and euthanasia and contrasts present viewpoints on these issues with the authority of the Bible.
    1. Sociology, Christian. 2. Ethics in the Bible.
3. Bible—Authority, evidences, etc.
[1. Christian life. 2. Conduct of life. 3. Ethics.
4. Bible—Authority, evidences, etc.] I. Title.
BT738.C698   241   81-16623
ISBN 0-87239-480-8   AACR2

Printed in U.S.A.   1982

TABLE OF CONTENTS

1. Authority 5
2. The Purpose of Government 15
3. Responsibilities of Citizenship 25
4. Socio-political Action 35
5. God of Life, God of Justice 45
6. Capital Punishment 53
7. War 65
8. Abortion..................................... 75
9. Euthanasia 85
10. Human Engineering 95
11. Racism 105
12. Anger 113
13. Pride 121

Authority

"Try to make us!"

I remember the incident well. We were in junior high school at the time. It happened during recess, when some of us were playing around at basketball in the gym. We had not been playing long when the coach of the junior-high basketball team blew his whistle and said, "Clear the floor! The team has to practice now."

There was no little resentment among us as we grudgingly yielded the floor to the privileged athletes. One of the disenfranchised non-jocks expressed his feelings by mumbling, "Try to make us!" He really didn't intend this for the coach's ears. He wasn't challenging; he was just grumbling. Unfortunately for him, he grumbled just loud enough for the coach to hear.

The gym got very quiet as the coach slowly walked over to face the cringing boy. In a stern tone he said, " 'Try to make us,' you say? Well, listen here, young man: don't think I *can't* make you. You'll do as I tell you. Now shape up and sit still!" He did. He was very still indeed.

That day the boy learned—we *all* learned—a lesson in authority. Despite the widespread attitude to the contrary, it is a fact that there are others who have the right to tell us what to do and to make us do it. In other words, there is such a thing as *authority*.

Authority is exactly this: it is the right to tell others what they ought to do, and the right to enforce the prescribed conduct through the use of power (such as the threat of punishment for contrary behavior).

The important word is *right*. A person has authority over me not just because he is bigger or smarter than I am, or because he has a gun in his hand, or because he is a forceful leader. Authority is a spiritual quality, an intangible moral *right,* which a person possesses with no necessary connection to his other qualities. Might does not make right in any true sense. A bully or a man with a gun may have the *power* to make me do something, but that doesn't give him the right to do so. On the other hand, a person may have the *right* to prescribe and enforce conduct, but may not have the power to do it. I remember a petite widowed mother of three strapping adolescent boys. Whenever the boys chose to defy their mother, there was no way she could make them obey. She just was not big enough. Does this mean that she had lost her authority as a parent? No! The authority to require obedience from her sons was still there, and even the right to enforce it remained, though she did not have the physical strength to do so.

Authority and morality go hand in hand. There is little need to seek the answers to ethical questions if one does not understand the nature of authority. Authority is the framework within which ethical decisions are made and moral conduct realized. Without authority, the whole concept of right and wrong is meaningless.

Thus in a book such as this, which deals with ethical problems, it is necessary to begin with a study of authority.

I. The Rejection of Authority

One of the most pervasive and most tragic characteristics of modern times is antiauthoritarianism, or the rejection of authority in favor of autonomy. As *Time* magazine once said, "Authority, the spirit of do it my way, is the clearly identified villain of education (and everything else) nowadays" (October 2, 1972, page 81).

A famous woman athlete has confessed to having a homosexual affair. Many are rushing to her defense. "She has the right to choose her own life-style," they say. "Everybody has the right to his own sexual preferences."

The "pro-choice" movement vehemently opposes all laws against abortion. "A woman has the right to do whatever she wants with her own body," they say.

Civil libertarians defend pornography and oppose all censorship. "A person has the right to read or watch whatever he wants to," they say.

These examples are expressions of autonomy, which is the enemy of authority. This word comes from two Greek words: *autos,* meaning "self," and *nomos,* meaning "law." The idea is that of self-rule, of being a law to oneself. A more common term is the word *freedom*.

A humanistic philosopher named James Christian describes autonomy as being free to make one's own decisions about what is right and what is wrong. Such decisions will differ from person to person, since they are based on the individual's private perception of his personal needs and nature, which in turn is based only on one's personal experience. To Mr. Christian this is highly superior to an authority relationship, where a person accepts someone else's (such as God's) decisions about right and wrong.

Mr. Christian makes this point in a book called *Philosophy: An Introduction to the Art of Wondering* (third edition: New York: Holt, Rinehart, and Winston, 1981; pages 109, 325). This book is used by many colleges as a basic textbook, instilling the concept of autonomy into the minds of many youth.

Such rebellion against authority pervades every aspect of modern culture. The *Humanist Manifesto II* (1973) asserts that "ethics is *autonomous* and *situational*, needing no theological . . . sanction." The countercultural *Yippie Manifesto* said, "We are all our own leaders." One of John Lennon's albums deals with kids in school. Lennon described its purpose thus: "I'd like to incite people to break the framework, to be disobedient in school, to stick their tongues out, to keep insulting authority."

Sylvia Ashton-Warner describes her experience in a "progressive" school where five-year-olds were taught autonomy and the full equality of teachers and students. Students were not made to do anything. A typical incident was as follows:

Teacher: "What about picking up your blocks?"
Henry: "I dowanna . . . and I don't have to."
Teacher: "Well, who else is to pick them up?"
Henry: "Not me, you dum-dum." (*Time,* op. cit.)

The Ohio Department of Education funded a study guide called *Education in Human Sexuality,* to be used in Ohio high schools. It teaches total autonomy in the area of ethics: "Moral behavior is behavior the individual feels is 'good' and immoral behavior is behavior the individual feels is 'bad' " (p. 84). "By definition, behavior you believe to be moral is moral and behavior you believe to be immoral is immoral, as you personally define and use your own values. . . . Every person has the right to his own concept of sexual morality" (p. 89).

It is no wonder that a Cincinnati high-school senior was quoted in the newspaper as saying, "If we are going to have morals, let's have personal ones. People should make their own rules."

To the modern mind, such absolute autonomy or freedom is a right to be demanded. Authority, law, obedience, and submission are evil concepts. They are repressive and oppressive. Rousseau lamented, "Man is born free, yet we see him everywhere in chains." To break the "chains" of authority is a high-priority goal for many today.

II. The Recovery of Authority

How should Christians respond to this antiauthoritarian trend? We must resist it! We must resist it with all the force we can muster. Above all else we have to be very careful that we ourselves are not seduced by the strong appeal of autonomy. Its satanic propaganda is everywhere: in the schools, in the media, in entertainment, in every aspect of culture. We must take care that we do not unconsciously begin to think in these terms, and we must help our children to perceive the dangers of this current attack on authority.

But we must do more. Christians must take an active role in a strong effort to recover the validity of the concepts of authority and submission in the world today. We ourselves must clearly understand the necessity of certain structures of authority, and we must do our best to get this point across in the face of strong opposition.

Why is the recovery of authority so urgent? Because, paradoxically, our freedom depends upon it. If everyone acted only from love and good will, it is conceivable that absolute autonomy in the area of morality would have no ill effects on society in general. But this is not the way things are. All men are sinners (Romans 3:23), and the hearts of sinners are usually filled with selfishness, greed, and hatred. If everyone were free to make his own rules and do anything he wanted, only the strongest and the meanest would *enjoy* such "freedom." The rest of us would live in fear and peril. We would not really be free at all.

For instance, if speed maniacs were free to barrel down the highway at 120 miles per hour without restraint, they would endanger themselves as well as others. If industrialists were free to dispose of toxic and chemical wastes in the air or in the nearest lake or stream without regulation and restraint, our health and lives would be threatened. If criminals were free to rob and extort without fear of punishment, the whole fabric of society would be torn asunder.

One does not have to be a Christian to realize this. The folk philosopher Eric Hoffer has said, "The average intellectual contrasts authority and freedom. I say that freedom is *impossible* without authority. The absence of authority is anarchy—and anarchy is a thousand-headed tyrant."

The Christian is interested in the recovery of authority not just for pragmatic reasons, though. We are concerned to reestablish respect for authority mainly because it is *right*. The basic fact of our existence is that we are *creatures* living in a God-created world. God as Creator and Lord of all has absolute authority; we as His creatures have an absolute obligation to submit to His authority. This is the only right thing to do; all desire for autonomy is evil as well as unnatural (i.e., against our nature as creatures).

God has not only made a world of creatures who must submit to Him; He has also established within the world a number of authority-relationships wherein human beings must submit to one another. Since these relationships are a part of our God-ordained existence, it is *right* that we acknowledge them and learn to live under authority.

These are the reasons why Christians should be concerned with the recovery of authority. By this time we can see how to accomplish this goal. The reality and proper role of authority will be recovered only when we recover the concept of God as Creator and Lord of the universe, and the concept of man as a creature of God.

The rejection of authority is rooted ultimately in the rejection of God. Thus we must call upon the world to acknowledge the real existence of the God who has revealed himself in Biblical history and in the pages of the Bible, and we must insist on the truth of Genesis 1:1, "In the beginning God created the heavens and the earth." Real authority, i.e., the moral right to tell others how to act, does not exist apart from God, and the fact that He has created everything from nothing is what gives Him this right. Psalms 24:1, 2 says,

> The earth is the Lord's, and all it contains,
> The world, and those who dwell in it.
> For He has founded it upon the seas,
> And established it upon the rivers.

Psalms 100:3 adds, "Know that the Lord Himself is God; it is He who has made us, and not we ourselves."

As a corollary to this, acceptance of authority depends on our understanding ourselves to be God's creatures. If we think of the human race as having evolved quite by accident, then there can be no such thing as a moral imperative handed down by someone who is "over" us. We have no master, and no one among us has the right to claim authority over another. This is one reason why the theory of evolution is so fanatically defended in spite of evidence to the contrary. If man is merely the accidental product of blind evolutionary forces, then he can justify his rejection of authority.

On the other hand, if we are creatures made by God for His purposes, then we are by nature under His authority. Submission and obedience are not unnatural, but are part of our essence; we cannot achieve authentic existence without them. If we are creatures, then absolute freedom is literally impossible. The one who asserts his autonomy is deceiving himself; he cannot possibly "uncreate" himself.

For our own good, then, and for the good of society in general, we must work for the recovery of authority. This means that we must acknowledge God as Creator and ourselves as His creatures, and we must lead others to do the same.

III. The Relationships of Authority

Inherent, absolute authority belongs only to God. He alone determines what His creatures ought and ought not to do. He alone declares what is moral and immoral, good and bad, right and wrong. By right of creation He imposes His will upon us, and we have no legitimate choice but to accept it. (Of course, we have freedom of will in the sense that we are free to do either right or wrong, but we are *not* free to decide what *is* right and what *is* wrong. This is God's prerogative.)

A. Divine Authority

Thus the basic relationship of authority is the one between us and God. We should submit ourselves to Him in all things. In the Christian era this involves submitting to the lordship of Jesus Christ, "for in Him all the fulness of Deity dwells in bodily form" (Colossians 2:9). He is God incarnate, God the Son; thus He shares the absolute authority of God the Father. As He says, "All authority has been given to Me in heaven and on earth" (Matthew 28:18).

Among other things, then, the Christian life is an authority relationship. Becoming a Christian means accepting the lordship of Jesus over our lives. We make the "good confession" that Jesus is Lord (see John 20:28; Romans 10:9). This means that we acknowledge Him as our owner and ourselves as His slaves. We commit ourselves to accept His instructions about what is sin and what is righteousness, and we commit ourselves to walk in the way of righteousness as He defines it.

This, of course, makes the Bible indispensable, since the written Word is the means by which God's authoritative instruction comes to us. "All Scripture is inspired by God and profitable for teaching, for reproof, for correction, for training in righteousness" (2 Timothy 3:16). It speaks to us with divine authority.

B. Delegated Authority

We are familiar with the idea of *delegated* authority. This means that the one in charge appoints someone else to act in his place in seeing that his orders are carried out. This is exactly what God has done as the means of maintaining order in the world. He has delegated His own authority to certain people.

This does not mean God has given them the right to make up their own rules. They are still bound by what He has revealed in Scripture, though they have the authority to say how God's rules shall be applied in particular cases. The main point, though, is that those to whom God has delegated His authority have the responsibility of requiring and enforcing obedience to God's rules, within specified limits.

God has established three spheres of authority, three distinct relationships within which certain ones are given an authority to which the rest must submit. These spheres are the family, the church, and the state. Within each of these units God has ordained that certain ones will be responsible for enforcing right conduct, and He has commanded the rest to submit to them.

The family is clearly an authority relationship. God has appointed parents to act for Him in instructing their children in the ways of righteousness. See Deuteronomy 6:4-9. To children He says, "Children, obey your parents in the Lord, for this is right" (Ephesians 6:1).

The church likewise is an authority relationship, with the elders in each local congregation being appointed to rule, to lead, and to guide. The rest of the congregation are required to submit to their authority: "Obey your leaders, and submit to them" (Hebrews 13:17).

The third sphere is the state, within which God has delegated His authority to those who occupy the offices of civil government. To the rest of us God says, "Let every person be in subjection to the governing authorities" (Romans 13:1). The implications of this relationship will be spelled out in greater detail in the next few chapters.

The Purpose of Government

Is capital punishment moral or immoral?
Is participation in warfare right or wrong?
What about huge funds for national defense?
Can a Christian be a policeman?
How can we know we are voting for the right candidate in an election?

These are serious questions, and quite controversial, too. Even Christians disagree over the answers. Why should this be? What is the source of confusion here? I believe that the basic problem is a failure to understand the purpose of human government. If a person has a wrong idea of what government is supposed to do, he should not be surprised to find himself in error concerning capital punishment, war, economic issues, and politics in general. The *purpose of government* is the key.

Why do we have human government, anyway? Is there a single correct answer to this question? Didn't government just evolve out of human need, and doesn't it operate by arbitrary consensus? No! Absolutely not! The

Bible tells us that God has ordained human government (Romans 13:1), and He has done so for a specific reason. Government thus has a God-ordained purpose, a God-appointed task to fulfill; and we are told what that purpose is in the New Testament. We need to read and respect the Word of God.

For a long time many people, including many Christians, have had the idea that religion and politics do not mix. In fact, it has been assumed that one's religion should remain somewhat isolated from the rest of his life altogether. Such an idea is tragically false, and we can rejoice that it is slowly but surely being rejected.

The truth is that Biblical "religion" (if we can call it that) was never meant to be just one aspect of a person's life. Commitment to Christ and His Word is a total way of life, a world-view. *Every* aspect of a Christian's life is "religious." The Bible contains authoritative teaching not only about "Sunday church," but also about politics, economics, education, family life, and daily work. We cannot presume to formulate opinions about any aspect of life and morality until we have examined what the Bible has to say about it.

This definitely applies to issues relating to politics and government, such as the ones named at the beginning of this chapter. And the starting point for understanding them all is the Bible's teaching about the purpose of government.

I. What Does The Bible Say?

Romans 13:1 says, "Let every person be in subjection to the governing authorities." It is generally agreed that Paul is talking here about civil government. This includes lawmakers such as representatives and councilmen, and more specifically the laws they enact. It also includes law-enforcement and peace-keeping personnel such as soldiers, policemen, and judges. (Titles and procedures differ from place to place.)

It will be remembered that civil government is one of the three spheres of authority established by God himself. Romans 13:1 says in full, "Let every person be in subjection to the governing authorities. For there is no authority except from God, and those which exist are established by God." This does not mean that God deliberately chooses every individual king, president, or sheriff. It means that every legitimate *kind* of authority has been instituted by God, including *civil* authority. God has ordained that there should be such a thing as human government, and He has commanded every person to submit to its authority. Jesus voiced this divine ordinance when He said, "Render to Caesar the things that are Caesar's" (Matthew 22:21).

The specific purpose and function of government can be learned by a study of three brief passages of Scripture: Romans 13:3-5; 1 Peter 2:13, 14; and 1 Timothy 2:1-4. (We do not look to the Old Testament for guidance here because of the unique nature of Israel's role as a nation.)

The basic passage is Romans 13:3-5. It reads, "For rulers are not a cause of fear for good behavior, but for evil. Do you want to have no fear of authority? Do what is good, and you will have praise from the same: for it is a minister of God to you for good. But if you do what is evil, be afraid; for it does not bear the sword for nothing; for it is a minister of God, an avenger who brings wrath upon the one who practices evil. Wherefore it is necessary to be in subjection, not only because of wrath, but also for conscience' sake."

Civil rulers are here called ministers of God. God has delegated His own authority to them; they act for Him and in His stead. Of course, civil authorities can and often do abuse their authority and act contrary to their ordained purpose. In such cases they are not *true* ministers, just as a preacher who perverts the gospel is not a true minister. Thus it is especially important for those involved in civil government to know what they are supposed to be doing.

What does Romans 13 say? The key words here are *fear, avenger,* and *wrath*. It would seem that the government's primary purpose is to *cause fear* in relation to evil behavior. The good citizen should not have to fear the law, but the evildoer *should* be afraid. "For rulers are not a cause of fear for good behavior, but for evil. . . . But if you do what is evil, be afraid." Afraid of what? The judicial punishment specified for evil behavior. A government whose legal and judicial system is such that it strikes fear in the heart of a potential criminal and deters his evil action is fulfilling its God-given purpose.

Deterring criminal behavior is not an end in itself, however. In the final analysis, this is done for the *good* (i.e., for the protection) of the law-abiding citizen. Paul says that if you do what is good, civil authority "is a minister of God to you for good." This is the ultimate purpose of government—to protect good people from those who would do evil against them.

This is further spelled out in 1 Timothy 2:1-4: "First of all, then, I urge that entreaties and prayers, petitions and thanksgivings, be made on behalf of all men, for kings and all who are in authority, in order that we may lead a tranquil and quiet life in all godliness and dignity. This is good and acceptable in the sight of God our Savior, who desires all men to be saved and to come to the knowledge of the truth."

Here Paul instructs us to pray for "all who are in authority." To what end? What should we pray that the authorities should be able to accomplish? He says we should pray for them "in order that we may lead a tranquil and quiet life in all godliness and dignity." Herein is specified the ultimate purpose of government: to provide an environment of peace and tranquility, free from threat of harm, where those who want to live a godly life can do so. (The reference to God's desire that all men be saved and know the truth implies that government should allow the gospel to be preached without hindrance.)

How can government provide such an environment? By the certain threat of just and swift punishment against those who do evil, as Romans 13 says.

In order to be effective in the deterrence of evil, the civil government has been authorized by God to punish those who actually commit crimes. As Paul says, "It is a minister of God, an avenger who brings wrath upon the one who practices evil" (Romans 13:4). The apostle Peter says the same thing: "Submit yourselves for the Lord's sake to every human institution, whether to a king as the one in authority, or to governors as sent by him for the punishment of evildoers and the praise of those who do right" (1 Peter 2:13, 14).

Since the ruler is acting for God, it is God's own wrath and vengeance that are enacted upon the criminal. God *could* wait until the Judgment Day to pour out His wrath; but in the interest of maintaining law and order in this world, He has appointed rulers to apply punishment now on His behalf.

It should be noted that deterrence of evil deeds is not the sole purpose of punishment. The government is an "avenger," and the punishment is "wrath." This means that the criminal is being punished because he *deserves* it. The punishment is vengeance; it is *retribution*. The New English Bible translates this part of Romans 13:4 thus: "They are God's agents of punishment, for retribution on the offender."

II. The Sum of It All: Justice

There is one word that sums up the purpose of government: JUSTICE. Justice is concerned with making sure that each person is treated strictly as he deserves: no more and no less.

Justice has two aspects, since what one deserves depends upon whether he is innocent or guilty in relation to the law. The *positive* aspect of justice, sometimes called distributive justice, relates to the innocent. It is basically the *protection* of the *rights* of the great mass of law-abiding citizens. Government's task is to insure justice for these by restraining evildoers who would violate their rights.

We should note that government's job is to *protect* our rights, not to *provide* everything we have a right to. Our basic right is the right to live a godly life in peace, unhindered and unthreatened, free from the fear of evildoers. (See 1 Timothy 2:1-4 again.) To this might be added a number of lesser rights, such as the right to own property, the right to self-improvement, the right to choose one's friends, and the right to negotiate for one's own employment (or employees, for that matter).

For an example, we might say that every person has the right to a college education. This does not mean that the government must *provide* it for everyone through financial grants. But if someone tries to interfere with anyone's right to a college education by unjust means such as racial discrimination, then government must step in to *protect* that right by making such discrimination illegal.

Regarding the *negative* aspect of justice, sometimes called retributive justice, the government's task is to see that the guilty get what *they* deserve, i.e., punishment. Some people think it is more noble or more "Christian" not to report a crime (even against oneself), or to try to abolish punishment altogether as a barbaric relic. But such decisions are misinformed and are a violation of justice. It definitely is wrong for an individual to seek his own revenge (Matthew 5:38, 39; Romans 12:19); but it is not wrong for civil authorities to arrest, try, and punish an evildoer. Indeed, they are not doing their job unless they do.

III. A Point of Confusion

The most serious misunderstanding of the purpose of government stems from a confusion of the roles of church and state. Just as the civil government has its Biblicallyrevealed purpose, so does the church. But the two are quite different. The contrast may be detailed as follows:

a. The *purpose* for which government exists is to maintain temporal law and order; the purpose for which the church exists is to provide spiritual salvation.
b. The *principle* by which government operates is justice; the principle by which the church operates is grace.
c. The *power* by which the state accomplishes its purpose is force; the power of the church is love.

Usually this is summarized in the simple contrast between justice and love. Government must see that justice prevails, while the church tries to change the world through love.

The confusion arises when these roles are reversed. Some well-meaning but misguided churchmen are declaring that the church's main task is the establishment of justice throughout the world. Likewise many are saying that all governmental policies, programs, and decisions must be determined by the love-ethic of Jesus as taught in Matthew 5:38-48.

As an example of the latter we may cite a recent president's attempt to establish a government of "love and compassion." Or we may call attention to a prominent senator who is convinced that our national and international political decisions must stem from a commitment to the power of love as the only means to any end. His own political activity, he says, is determined by "the character and quality of love I see in Christ."

Another example of this confusion of the roles of church and government comes from a magazine article published a number of years ago. A teacher was advocating a "way out" of the Viet Nam mess and war in general. His solution was for America to meet the aggressive overtures of the Communist world with "real" power—"the full power of love." He recommended "a foreign policy based on the principle of love," which our enemies could not resist. "Two hundred million Americans armed with God's love—the love that says I will give the other man what he needs, not what he deserves, because that is how God loves me—cannot be defeated." We should establish a new cabinet post, he said, "to implement a foreign policy based on the reality concept of Jesus; love is the only real power. I have faith that this choice will bring peace on earth."

Needless to say, at first glance this all sounds very good, very pious, and very Christian. *But it isn't!* What all of these men are describing is God's program for the *church,* not civil government. If our government attempted to follow these suggestions, it would be abdicating its God-given responsibility and abandoning its God-ordained purpose of implementing justice.

What are the sources of such confusion? One is the failure to recognize that Jesus' "love your enemies" teaching was never meant to be a mandate to civil government as such. It is the ethic of the kingdom of God, and is meant to be applied by individual Christians in their interpersonal relationships. The Biblical instruction for government is quite different.

Another source of confusion is an idealistic view of human nature that underestimates the power of evil in the hearts of sinners. The very rationale for civil government is the fact that the mass of evil men can be restrained *only* by fear and force. Certainly *some* will respond to the church's message of love, but *all* must be restrained by force in order to maintain peace while the gospel is being preached.

Idealistic approaches to government, those which assume that all evil men will respond to gestures of love and compassion, are doomed to fail. This is illustrated very well in the experience of criminology professor George Kirkham. As a college professor, he says, he had numerous encounters with convicted criminals in his air-conditioned office; and he found them all to be quite calm and reasonable. He was sure that policemen exaggerated the amount of violence and abuse they faced each day.

Kirkham decided, however, that he ought to get a firsthand impression of the situation; so he joined the police force. What he found shocked him. "Now, as a police officer," he says, "I began to encounter the offender for the first time as a very real menace to my personal safety and the security of our society. The felon was no longer a harmless figure sitting in blue denims across my prison desk, a 'victim' of society to be treated with compassion and leniency." What he saw was armed robbers waving guns; crazed maniacs threatening their families; hostile, cursing, stone-throwing crowds; and angry men swinging cues at each other in smoke-filled pool rooms.

His conclusion? "Whatever the risk to himself, every police officer understands that his ability to back up the lawful authority which he represents is the only thing which stands between civilization and the jungle of lawlessness." This is realism. This is why God gave us civil government.

IV. How Should We Vote?

The most practical way to apply all of this is in the voting booth. How do we decide which candidate to vote for? Basically we should vote for the one whose view of civil government comes closest to the Biblical teaching. Which one understands most clearly that government's job is to protect the rights of the innocent and to punish the guilty? How does he apply this understanding to such issues as national defense, law and order, capital punishment, abortion, labor unionism, reverse discrimination, environmental pollution, taxation, and welfare? Does he look upon government as a protector or as a provider of rights? Does he see government in terms of justice or in terms of "love and compassion"?

Note: whether that candidate is a Christian or not must not be the deciding factor in our choice. Many Christian politicians have a perverted understanding of the purpose of government and are not fit to hold civil office. We should not vote for a particular candidate *just* because he is a Christian. The candidate who wants government to do what *God* wants it to do is the one who should get our vote.

Responsibilities of Citizenship

There is another side to the coin. If there is government, there must also be the governed. Governors imply governees. And if God's Word gives us instructions about the responsibilities of the former, we can be assured that it also describes the responsibilities of the latter.

Relatively few of us will ever become kings, presidents, mayors, or policemen. However, almost one hundred percent of us are citizens of particular countries, among the *governed,* subject to the authority of civil rulers. In most cases rulers themselves are personally subject to the laws that they officially enact and administer. Thus we should all be keenly interested in what the Bible says about the responsibilities of citizenship.

I. Civil Obedience

What does it mean to live under civil authority? How does a Christian citizen respond to laws and decrees and regulations and judgments? Several Biblical commandments are applicable here, chief among which is the simple command to *obey the law*.

25

Civil obedience is clearly and undeniably a citizen's duty. Romans 13 says, "Let every person be in subjection to the governing authorities. For there is no authority except from God, and those which exist are established by God. Therefore he who resists authority has opposed the ordinance of God; and they who have opposed will receive condemnation upon themselves. . . . Wherefore it is necessary to be in subjection, not only because of wrath, but also for conscience' sake" (verses 1, 2, 5). First Peter 2:13, 14 echoes this command: "Submit yourselves for the Lord's sake to every human institution: whether to a king as the one in authority; or to governors as sent by him for the punishment of evildoers and the praise of those who do right."

Thus the absolute authority of God's Word instructs us to submit to the delegated authority of civil government. Since the decisions of civil government usually come to us in the form of laws, God is telling us to obey the laws of the land.

A. Motives for Obedience

Romans 13:5 gives us two reasons or motives for obeying the law. First, Paul says, we should be in subjection "because of wrath." What does he mean? He is referring to the government's duty to punish lawbreakers. The ruler is "an avenger who brings wrath upon the one who practices evil" (Romans 13:4). We should obey in order to escape this wrath, whether it be in the form of a thousand-dollar fine or a five-year jail sentence.

Obeying "because of wrath" may also refer to something infinitely more serious. We must remember that civil authorities operate as God's servants. God has ordained government, and He has ordained *obedience* to government. "Therefore he who resists authority has opposed the ordinance of God," says Romans 13:2; "and they who have opposed will receive condemnation upon themselves." It is likely that Paul is here referring to

God's final judgment and eternal wrath upon sinners. This is a severe warning! It shows us the seriousness of civil obedience. When one flouts the law of man, he is at the same time scoffing at the law of God. Disregard for civil authority signals lack of submission to God's own authority. What else can we expect, then, but condemnation? Thus we should strive to be in subjection "because of wrath."

Most of us are aware of the fact that fear of punishment is not an especially noble motive for obedience. It may be that this is often the only thing that will cause hardened hearts to keep the law, though. Thus laws must have penalties attached to them, and we must not forget this part of the picture. But God has specified in Romans 13:5 a second motive for civil obedience, namely, we should obey "for conscience' sake." This is by far the higher motive, and it is the one that should rule in the Christian's heart.

To obey "for conscience' sake" means to obey simply because it is right, simply because God wants us to and has commanded us to. Why should it have to be otherwise for one who loves God? If we know that this is what God wants, then we should make every effort to fulfill His desires. Isn't this the very nature of love, after all? The apostle Peter puts it succinctly when he says, "Submit yourselves *for the Lord's sake*" (1 Peter 2:13). Obeying to escape punishment is for our own sake, but obeying just because it is the right thing to do is for *God's* sake.

What practical difference does this make in one's life? Basically it means that we must obey every law and every ordinance of man, even when there is no policeman around and when there is no danger of being arrested or ticketed. Since fear of punishment is the *only* thing that motivates many people, then if they can be relatively sure they won't be caught, they will not hesitate to break any law they want to. But this *cannot* be the Christian's attitude! "For conscience' sake" and "for the Lord's sake" mean that we do not care whether there is a policeman around or not: we will obey anyway, just because it is right to obey and sinful to disobey.

I remember when the issue of civil obedience came up in a philosophy class at a secular university. As one of the students, I expressed the Biblical position as outlined above. The teacher replied incredulously, "Do you mean that if you were driving alone on a country road at three A.M. with not another soul within five miles, and if you came to a stop sign, you would actually *stop?*" "Of course," I said.

Now, I can understand why he had difficulty with this approach to law, since he had no regard for the authority of God's Word. What puzzles me is that many Christians, who have professed surrender to the lordship of Christ, look upon such an approach as peculiar and fanatical. Have they never read, "Be in subjection . . . for conscience's sake"?

B. Taking Obedience Seriously

There *is* an exception to a citizen's obligation to obey civil laws; it will be discussed below. Most acts of law-breaking do not fall within this excepted category, however. Most violations are nothing more than expressions of the sinful spirit of *autonomy*. The individual simply decides to put himself above the law. He decides that his actions will be determined not by law, but by his own desires. He will simply do whatever he wants to do, ignoring the law whenever he wants to and thinks he can get away with it.

Many Christians, unfortunately, have this very attitude. They justify their lawlessness with all sorts of feeble excuses. "That's not an important law." "Nobody got hurt." "Everybody does it." "I was in a hurry." "That's a stupid law." "It's for a good cause." "I needed the money." "It's just too much trouble." "I don't see what difference it makes."

Let's face it. Do we really think God is impressed with such wispy excuses? Do we really think God is pleased and honored by a church choir singing from Xeroxed copies of copyrighted music? Do preachers really think God laughs along with them as they joke about their reputations as chronic speeders? Do we really think God won't notice us in that crowd of jaywalkers ignoring the "WAIT" signal? Do we really think God admires our cleverness when we use radar detectors and CB radios to speed without getting caught?

There is NO justification for such a self-willed approach to law. God does not say, "Obey the laws—except when it's inconvenient. Obey the laws—except the ones you think are stupid. Obey the laws—except when it might cost you a little time or money. Obey the laws—except the little ones." God says simply, "Let every person be in subjection to the governing authorities." This includes all traffic and pedestrian laws, all building codes, all hunting and fishing laws, all tax laws, all copyright laws, and all littering laws. God commands us to obey them *all*.

By this time someone must be getting a bit agitated and must be muttering self-righteously about legalism and Christian freedom. This is because some have the mistaken notion that Christians under grace are no longer under obligation to obey rules or laws of any kind. They equate complete obedience with legalism, and condemn it. This is a very serious error, though. Christians are no longer under law *as a system of salvation,* but we are just as much obligated to obey every law that applies to us, including civil laws, as anyone ever was. Legalism is not law-keeping, but *depending* on law-keeping for salvation. When Jesus condemned the Pharisees for neglecting "the weightier provisions of the law" (justice, mercy, and faithfulness), He still warned them *not to neglect the little things* (tithing their mint leaves and garden seeds). See Matthew 23:23.

C. Taxes and Prayer

One aspect of civil obedience that requires special attention, since the Bible mentions it specifically, is paying taxes. In Romans 13, after outlining a government's responsibilities, Paul instructs the citizens to pay taxes in order to meet the operating costs. He says, "For because of this you also pay taxes, for rulers are servants of God, devoting themselves to this very thing. Render to all what is due them: tax to whom tax is due; custom to whom custom; fear to whom fear; honor to whom honor" (verses 6, 7).

When Jesus' enemies challenged Him concerning the propriety of paying taxes to Rome, He gave the reply, "Render to Caesar the things that are Caesar's; and to God the things that are God's" (Matthew 22:21). Here Jesus sanctions the right of government to levy taxes, and He enjoins citizens to pay them. Paying taxes is never pleasant, and we may not always agree with the way the government spends our money. But we should remember that no one has ever hated to pay taxes any more than the Jews hated to pay them to Rome. Yet Jesus left them with no loopholes. "Render to Caesar," He said. Do we think we have any better case against paying taxes than the Jews did? Of course not. Lying about income or expenses and thus cheating on our income tax is unconditionally sinful. A professing Christian who does this should reexamine his relation to God.

There is no justification, either, for withholding a part of our tax payment because we have a conscientious objection to the way some of it is spent. This is the spirit of anarchy. Do we think the Roman government never spent their tax revenues unwisely or immorally? Of course they did. The Caesars wasted monstrous amounts on debauchery, excess, and destruction. Yet Jesus said, "Render to Caesar." If we do not like the way the government is using our tax money, let us work for reform in the way it is spent. Withholding or evading taxes is sinful.

Another responsibility of Christian citizens is praying for our government. Paul says that we should pray "for kings and all who are in authority" (1 Timothy 2:1, 2). The basic content of these prayers should be that the various individuals with civil responsibilities will do their jobs in accordance with God's design, thus providing us with a quiet and peaceable environment.

The command to pray for rulers reminds us of the truth that God is in charge of the affairs of men and governments. He may permit them to go the way of their own freely-chosen folly, but He can intervene and alter circumstances if He so purposes. Let us not forget that our prayers may at times be a key factor in God's decision to intervene on our behalf.

II. Civil Disobedience

As was mentioned earlier, there is an exception to a citizen's obligation to obey the law. We must now examine the nature of that exception.

Even though civil rulers are ministers of God and have had authority delegated to them by God himself, their authority is not absolute. The reason for this is that they, like all human beings, are fallible and sinful. Thus they may, through bad judgment or malice, sometimes make laws that must be disobeyed. Once we grant this fact, we must be very careful to define the nature of such exceptions very clearly, since fallible and sinful citizens may use this principle to excuse unjustifiable disobedience to all sorts of laws.

Biblical teaching and examples seem to allow only one kind of civil disobedience, namely, in a case where obedience to a particular civil law would require us to *disobey* a law of God. The clearest example of this is in Acts 4 and 5, where Peter and the other apostles had to choose between obedience to Christ and obedience to the Jewish Sanhedrin. In order to curb the growth of the church, the Jewish rulers commanded Peter and John "not to speak or teach at all in the name of Jesus" (Acts 4:18). Peter and John gave a sound answer, saying, in effect, "Do you really think we ought to obey you rather than God?" (Acts 4:19). After all, they had specific instructions from Jesus to preach and teach in His name (Matthew 28:18-20; Acts 1:8). And so they continued to preach.

The Sandhedrin responded by arresting the apostles, but God sent an angel to deliver them from prison. They immediately resumed their preaching. When the authorities finally located them and brought them back before the council, the high priest said, "We gave you strict orders not to continue teaching in this name, and behold, you have filled Jerusalem with your teaching." The apostles replied simply, "We must obey God rather than men" (Acts 5:17-29).

A parallel incident may be found in Daniel 6, where Daniel's enemies, in order to get him arrested, persuaded the king to issue a decree that was in direct conflict with Daniel's obligation to God: all prayer, except to the king himself, was forbidden for thirty days. Of course Daniel chose to obey God rather than men, and his choice led to the lion's den.

If a Christian is faced with such a choice, he must follow the same course in spite of the consequences. At times, during the early days of the church, Christians were commanded to worship Caesar and curse Christ or else face death. See 1 Corinthians 12:3. Of course they had to disobey this edict. Many German Christians refused to fight in Hitler's unjust wars and were penalized. Some believe that Bible smuggling into Communist countries is justified, since we must obey the Great Commission rather than Russian smuggling laws. There may be different opinions in such cases.

There are times, however, when sincere people engage in civil disobedience for reasons certainly not sanctioned in the Bible. Some feel they are free to break any law they judge to be unjust and unfair. For instance, a commercial fisherman may feel it is unfair for the law to limit his daily catch of a certain kind of fish, so he regularly catches more than the limit and hides them from the inspector. This kind of civil disobedience cannot be justified, though, since compliance with this law—even if it *is* unjust—would in no way require the fisherman to sin. His personal judgment that the law is unfair does not relieve him from the obligation to obey it. There is no conflict between this law and the law of God.

Another common form of civil disobedience is motivated by the desire to make a forceful protest against some unacceptable circumstance. An individual or a group may choose to disobey a law that has nothing to do with the situation against which they are protesting, simply as a means of calling attention to themselves and their grievance. Some advocates of civil rights have been noted for this kind of civil disobedience in the form of unlawful marches and sit-ins. Truck drivers have resorted to traffic slowdowns (driving three abreast on an interstate highway at five miles per hour) to protest undesirable regulations.

In such cases the cause is often just; the grievance is real. But even where this is the case, *this still does not justify lawbreaking!* The laws in these cases usually have no direct connection with the problem. To resort to this method of protest is to say that the end justifies the means, which is another door to anarchy. The Bible simply does not condone this kind of civil disobedience.

The conclusion is that there is only one valid situation in which God permits us to break a civil law, namely, where obedience to the law would in itself cause us to sin against a law of God. In every other case, disobedience to civil law is *itself* a sin against God, and it is time for Christians to begin taking this seriously.

Socio-Political Action

Here is a week's calendar of activities for the First Secularian Church:

Mon. 7 p.m.—C.A.G.E. (Clamor About Genderial Equality) meets in the church auditorium. Mayor Jerry Faller will discuss hiring quotas for city jobs.
Tues. 8 a.m.—Bus leaves for nuclear power plant construction site. Picket signs provided.
Tues. 7 p.m.—O.I.L. (Objector's Information Lobby) will explain how to avoid the military draft if it is re-instituted.
Wed. 7 p.m.—Midweek study class: Chapter 4 of John Calvin Queen's book, *Using Civil Disobedience to Get What You Want*.
Thurs. 7 p.m.—Missionary meeting. Brother Jose Garcia will report on the land reform program to redistribute 50,000 acres in Colombia.
Sun. 10 a.m.—Morning worship: Reverend Jones and Councilman Bobby Pleasant will debate the issue of guaranteed annual income. (NOTE: the Lord's

Supper will be available in Classroom 22 for those who want it.)

The calendar of activities for Riverside Evangelistic Church is a bit different:

Mon. 7 p.m.—C.A.M.E. (Christians and Mass Evangelism) meets in the church auditorium. Reverend Jerry Springwell will discuss preparations for his coming evangelistic crusade.
Tues. 8 a.m.—Bus committee meets to discuss purchase of five new buses and development of five new Sunday morning routes.
Tues. 7 p.m.—G.A.S. (God's Army of Soulwinners) meets to study techniques of door-to-door calling in high-rise apartments.
Wed. 7 p.m.—Midweek study class: Chapter 4 of Evangelist Billy Grayveal's *99 New Ways to Win Souls*.
Thurs. 7 p.m.—Missionary committee meeting. Brother Kim Lee will report on the program to start 50 new churches in Korea this year.
Sun. 10 a.m.—Morning worship: Reverend Smith will preach on "Win a Soul or Lose Your Own." (NOTE: A box will be available in Classroom 22 for donating worn-out clothing to City Mission.)

These exaggerated calendars reflect some of the strong disagreement within Christendom regarding the purpose of the church, especially regarding social problems. We saw above that it is the task of civil government to eliminate injustice and implement justice. But the question must still be asked, what responsibility does the church have in these areas?

This question is usually asked regarding a whole category of problems listed under the general heading of "social injustice." This includes such things as poverty, racism, poor housing, disease, militarism, war, and environmental pollution. Carl Henry lists the following as especially relevant concerns for today: "the primacy of the family . . . the dignity and worth of fetal life, the plight of the poor and oppressed, the right and need to work, the pursuit of world peace and order, the just use of power to contain the expansionist policies of aggressor nations, and the preservation of natural resources" (*Christianity Today,* Oct. 24, 1980, p. 25).

Activity directed toward solving such problems is usually called "socio-political action." Should the church engage in such activity? Should social reform and political projects be on the church's agenda? Is the elimination of social injustice and temporal human misery any business of the church? This chapter will suggest an answer to this question.

I. Social Injustice

We must first explain the nature of the problem in more detail. Exactly what is "social injustice"? First it must be distinguished from *personal* sins, which have been the traditional target of ecclesiastical wrath, such as drinking, gambling, adultery, and greed. These are still sins, of course, and the church still opposes them. But they are individual problems and are usually solved by personal repentance.

By contrast, social injustice has to do with what are called systemic sins or societal sins. It focuses not so much on the wrongness of individual acts as on the wrongness of economic or political systems as such, the injustice of sociological patterns and structures of society. Christians may disagree about these.

For instance, an individual's greed may lead him to steal from his neighbor, but (as some see it) the capitalistic system as such steals from the worker and must be abolished. (As others see it, the *socialistic* system, which redistributes wealth via taxation and welfare, steals from the worker and must be opposed.)

Other examples of social structures that some consider sinful are entrenched racism, multinational corporations, communism, big business, the military machine, the nuclear energy lobby, labor unionism, the advertising industry (for encouraging excessive consumption), and the entertainment industry (for glorifying immorality).

To label such impersonal structures and systems unjust and sinful does not do away with personal responsibility in connection with them. Such systems could not exist apart from the individuals who originate, perpetuate, and tolerate them; and those who do so incur personal guilt if the systems really are evil. The point is, however, that if the systems *themselves* are evil, then social injustice cannot be corrected until the systems are changed.

Another distinction must be made between the *causes* and the *effects* of social injustice. The causes are the corrupt systems such as were listed above. The effects are the various kinds of suffering and misery that abound in the world today.

Each of these views is held by some: capitalism leads to poverty by concentrating property in the hands of a few; racism leads to discrimination, which in turn leads to humiliation and economic suffering; labor union extortion (i.e., strikes) fuels inflation and steals from everyone; big business pollutes with impurity and endangers our health; the military machine in action causes untold misery and destruction; even when dormant it increases poverty by draining resources away from the needy; and television helps corrupt the morals of the nation by glorifying just about everything the Bible condemns.

To quote a typical mass-mailed social-action letter, "*Ten million Third World babies are starving* because of the heartless, money-hungry actions of powerful multinational corporations. *Only you can stop the scandal!*" Who is doing this despicable thing? Why, corporations such as the Nestlé Company. How? By promoting and selling powdered infant formula in Haiti, Nigeria, and elsewhere. How can we act? By boycotting Nestlé products, writing to the company, and sending ten or a hundred dollars to INFACT (Infant Formula Action Coalition). Dr. Spock and the National Council of Churches urge us to do it.

Whether the particular accusation is justified or not, the point is that social injustice has both its causes and its effects. The main target of socio-political action is usually the *causes,* not the effects. The goal is to eliminate poverty and suffering, but the means of doing so is to eradicate the causes: the societal structures that are thought to be sinful.

II. The Church's Role: Three Views

If you or your church had received the letter from INFACT mentioned above, what would you have done? Would you have ignored it? Would you have privately resolved to forgo Nestlé's *Quik* and chocolate chip cookies? Would you have organized your Sunday-school class or the whole church to engage in such a boycott? Or would you have concluded, as some did, that Nestlé's formula really is a help to millions of third-world babies?

Exactly what must be the church's approach to sociopolitical action? There are three main answers to this question. They are discussed more fully in John Stott's book, *Christian Mission in the Modern World* (IVP 1975), chapter 1. The first view is that the church should *never* engage in social action. Its only task is evangelism—"proclaiming the gospel to individuals"—and it should concentrate on that alone. The second parody of a church calendar at the beginning of this chapter typifies this view.

The second view goes to the other extreme, namely, that the church's *only* mission is social action. This is usually the approach of liberal churches that have rejected the Biblical teaching on sin, Christ, salvation, Heaven, and Hell and thus have no gospel to preach anyway. One liberal theologian describes the church's mission as being "concerned with the overcoming of industrial disputes, with the surmounting of class divisions, with the eradication of racial discrimination." Another says, "Contemporary evangelism is moving away from winning souls one by one, to the evangelism of the structures of society." The calendar of the "First Secularian Church" above reflects this view. Its program reveals no concern about redeeming individuals one by one from sin and death.

The third view is that both evangelism and social action are necessary parts of the church's mission. Any church that loves Jesus and loves the lost and needy cannot exclude either one from its agenda.

Most churches probably are in the third category, but within this view there is still a sharp division regarding the *relationship* between evangelistic and social work. On the the one hand, many believe that these two aspects are of equal importance or that each is an end in itself. This is John Stott's view. He says, "*Social action is a partner of evangelism.* . . . Each stands on its own feet in its own right alongside the other. . . . For each is an end in itself" (*Christian Mission*, p. 27). According to Ronald Sider, Jesus gave both equal time during His ministry. There is no hint "that Jesus considered healing sick people any less important than preaching the Good News. He commanded us *both* to feed the hungry *and* to preach the Gospel" (*Christianity Today*, Oct. 8, 1976, pp. 28, 29).

On the other hand, many who see both evangelistic and social work as necessary do not see them as equal partners. Instead they maintain that evangelism is the primary task of the church, and that social action is to be undertaken mainly as one *means* toward accomplishing that task. Some criticize this view, saying this makes social work arise from an ulterior motive and thus lack sincerity. Stott rejects it, saying that in this case "the smell of hypocrisy hangs round our philanthropy" (p. 26).

III. A Suggested Biblical Program

In this last section we will defend a specific position on this issue of the church's involvement in socio-political action. Our view is closest to but not identical with the last one described above.

I strongly believe that the church's primary task is evangelizing the lost according to the program of the Great Commission: proclaiming the gospel, baptizing those who accept it, and nurturing them to mature and abundant life in Christ.

I believe that this position is true to the teaching of the New Testament. The ministry and teaching of Jesus especially support this view, in spite of all efforts to make our Lord a model for the equal-role view of social action. We should not pervert Jesus' quotation of Isaiah 61:1, 2 by making it refer only to physical poverty, blindness, and captivity (Luke 4:18, 19). Yes, Jesus healed the blind and fed the hungry, but this is not why He came. God could have sent an angel or empowered a prophet to do such things if these were ends in themselves. But Jesus came to do what *no one else* could do: "The Son of Man has come to seek and to save that which was lost" (Luke 19:10). He came to redeem us with His blood. He healed the blind and lame as a means to an end: to lead people to trust Him as their Savior so that He could heal their spiritual blindness and liberate them from sin's bonds. See Mark 2:10, 11; John 20:30, 31.

This does not mean that justice is in a state of limbo as far as the church is concerned. It means simply that we recognize that God has created a division of labor. The church is in charge of evangelism; and *the government is in charge of justice,* as we saw in chapter 2.

To say that the church's *principal* purpose is evangelism does not mean that it has no secondary responsibilities. In fact, socio-political action *is* one of the church's tasks. Yes, the church *should* attack social injustice, in both its causes and its effects. But this is *not* a task equal to evangelism, and in many cases is done as a means to evangelism.

The following is a suggested program for the church's involvement in socio-political activity.

A. *Indirect* Action Against the *Causes*

The church as church does not become directly involved in political affairs; it does not directly attack the sinful social structures that cause injustice. But it may and should take *indirect* action to bring about fundamental changes in society.

First of all, *evangelism* itself is an indirect way—probably the best way—of changing society. After all, since societal ills are caused by people, societal reform must begin with *people*. The best way to persuade people to abandon unjust ways is to change their hearts through the gospel. The more faithful the church is to its main task of evangelism, the faster the causes of injustice disappear.

A second indirect approach is this: the church should *encourage* its individual members to become directly involved in the political process. Christians as citizens can and should become politically active, lobbying for justice and seeking public office. Christians can act individually, or they can join organizations (e.g., the Right to Life Committee, Common Cause, the Conservative Caucus, the Moral Majority, or INFACT) if they feel sure those organizations are really fighting real injustice, and doing it in proper ways.

A third means of indirect action is the church's fulfillment of its responsibility to be the *conscience of society*. One of the church's tasks has always been to speak out against sin of all kinds and to call the world to righteousness. This is part of the task of evangelism, since turning to Christ involves turning away from sin. Also, our sincere concern for those suffering the misery of injustice motivates us to speak out against the particular kinds of sin that cause it.

But even apart from these considerations, it is the church's prophetic task to be the conscience of society, to condemn sin and proclaim holiness. A major aspect of this task is to remind civil authorities of *their* responsibility to seek justice. Christians may not always agree as to what constitutes injustice and proper remedial action, but when there is a clear issue between right and wrong, it is *right* and *necessary* to speak out.

What are some methods by which the church can make its voice heard? Sermons from the pulpit, later published in the local paper or sent to public officials, can be effective. Organized letter-writing to newspapers or senators, organized picketing of abortion chambers or porno shops, and organized boycotts can all be effective. One local minister organized a telephone campaign against X-rated movies in his community. It worked.

B. *Direct* Action Against the *Effects*

The church also must engage in direct social action in relation to the effects of injustice. It must be *directly* involved in relieving the misery and suffering of individuals. This involves benevolent activity of three kinds.

First is a program of *brotherhood* benevolence, directed toward those within the church who are in need. We are directed, as much as we are able, to meet the needs of "the household of the faith" first of all (Galatians 6:10). The use of the word *brothers* in Matthew 25:40 and 1 John 3:17, 18 suggests care for Christ's people. The examples of benevolence in the early church were limited to the needy among the faithful. See Acts 2:44-46; 4:34, 35; 6:1-6; 11:29, 30; 1 Corinthians 16:1-3. A contemporary example would be the sponsoring of a Christian refugee family.

A second kind of benevolence is *occasional* benevolence directed toward unbelievers in emergency situations. The pattern for this is the Good Samaritan; in cases of emergency no questions are asked about a person's faith. See Galatians 6:10 again. It directs us to help "all men" as the opportunity arises.

The third kind is *evangelistic* benevolence, or helping the poor and needy as a means of opening their hearts to the gospel. This should be done in the local community; it should be and is being done on the mission field with great effectiveness (e.g., via hospitals, orphanages, and schools). Such works of love are no more hypocritical than were Jesus' miracles of healing, where the primary purpose was to bring unbelievers to faith. (See Matthew 5:16 also.)

If a church follows this program, it should have a clear conscience with regard to socio-political action.

God of Life, God of Justice

The very presence of life on our planet is a marvel that too often goes unappreciated. In this connection it is edifying to meditate on one of the more significant results of our space program: the close-up pictures of the surface of the moon and of Mars. Why are these pictures significant? Because they show the absolute contrast between our living earth and the stark, utterly barren *deadness* that prevails elsewhere.

The abundance and variety of living things here on earth stagger the imagination. Everywhere we go we are literally surrounded by life: on the highest mountains, in the deepest oceans, in every nook and cranny of land, in the stratosphere, and even in the "Dead" Sea! Estimates of the total number of animal and plant species range from two million to four and a half million. (Estimates of the number of *extinct* species range as high as sixteen *billion*.)

Among these millions (billions?) of kinds of life, one stands out far above all the rest in significance and uniqueness, namely, *human* life. It is a phenomenon without parallel, a source of endless awe and fascination.

Our interest in the subject is a very practical one, since quite a number of the most serious ethical problems are literally matters of human life and death. Our approach to these problems depends on our understanding of life. Thus before we can proceed to a discussion of war, capital punishment, abortion, euthanasia, and other issues, we must see what the Bible says about the nature and value of human life, especially in its relation to justice.

I. The Nature of Human Life

Looking first at the nature of human life, we note the basic truth that man is a *God-created* being, not a product of chance evolution. The Biblical summary of creation (Genesis 1:1—2:7) tells us that the whole universe was planned and produced by God, according to His design and for His purpose. This includes the human race: "And God created man in His own image" (Genesis 1:27).

That God created man means that God is the sole Lord of human life. The Maker lays down the rules for that which He makes. The Potter has authority over the clay. Thus it is God, through His Word, who tells us what is right and wrong with regard to the treatment of human life.

That God created man means also that man's basic design has already been determined by God, and we are not at liberty to experiment with new models. God made us the way He wants us to be. We are not just a transient stage in the process of evolution, subject to manipulation and "improvement," capable of directing our own evolution now that we have accidentally acquired intelligence.

Another point about the nature of human life is that it is *dual*, i.e., it has two aspects, the physical and the spiritual. God made man's body from the common elements of the earth (Genesis 2:7); then He added the personal spirit or soul, which is qualitatively different from the material part. Thus man has *physical* life, which is similar to animal life in general. He also has *spiritual* life, which can exist apart from the physical but is not intended to. Both aspects are God-created, and both are necessary to the full humanness of man.

The reference to man's spirit leads to another point about human life, namely, that man as spirit is created in *God's image*. After all else had been created by simple fiat ("Let there be . . ."), God paused in self-deliberation and said, "Let Us make man in Our image, according to Our likeness" (Genesis 1:26). This solemn declaration of intent was followed by the act (Genesis 1:27). God brought into existence an earthly creature who is also spirit, and who is thus able to fellowship with divine Spirit.

It is man's spirit, not his body, that is in God's image. The basic characteristic of spirit is personhood. Man, like God, is personal. This means not only that he has self-consciousness, but also that he has the capacity for *God*-consciousness. Man as personal spirit is able to know and commune with the divine persons.

The final point about the nature of man should be obvious: human life is absolutely *unique*. It is qualitatively different from all other creation and all other forms of life. Of course, it is the spiritual, personal life of man that sets him apart from animal and plant life as such. Of all earthly creatures, only man is in God's image. He is in a category by himself.

Let us not misunderstand the special nature of man's life. Being spirit is what makes him special, but it is not just man's spiritual life that is unique. Because man is spirit—in God's image—*even his physical life is unique and qualitatively different*. Man is not just a part of some vast evolutionary continuum, not even on the physical level. The physical life of animals may indeed be just a function of certain electro-chemical processes (which may even be duplicated in a laboratory someday). But *human* physical life is inseparable from the presence of the human spirit: "The body without the spirit is dead" (James 2:26).

Actually, even though it is possible to think of man's spiritual life and his physical life separately (Matthew 10:28), it is best to speak simply of *human* life—life which is special in every way.

II. The Value of Human Life

Because of the nature of man as being in God's image and thus unique, God has put an extremely high value on human life. Of all the tangible things that exist in the universe, human beings are the most important. Human life is of more inherent worth than all the gold and jewels and money one can imagine, of more value than all the galaxies combined.

Two things demonstrate to us the high value of human life. One is the sixth commandment, Exodus 20:13, "You shall not murder" ("Thou shalt not kill," as the King James Version has it). God has protected human life with this solemn prohibition. He has warned us that murderers will not inherit the kingdom of God (Galatians 5:21, KJV), but will wind up in the lake of fire, which is the second death (Revelation 21:8).

Some people follow a philosophy called "reverence for life," advocated by Albert Schweitzer. Schweitzer had a mystical regard for all life as something sacred, something to be revered. His policy was to respect all living things alike, including men, germs, thistles, seals, whales, snakes, and mosquitoes. He rejected any inherent distinction between "higher and lower" life, "more valuable and less valuable" life. He did his best to avoid killing anything, even a fly, unless it was a threat to man. He regretted having to sacrifice the life of sleeping sickness germs in order to save human life.

To some Christians this may sound like a very admirable concept, one derived from Exodus 20:13 itself. This is not the case, however. It is *not* a Biblical philosophy, but a *pagan* one, consistent only with such systems as Hindu monism or chance evolution. Surely all of God's creation deserves our respect, and we treat none of it with indifference. But to say that no kind of life—including human life—is more valuable than another is a blatant denial of God's Word. Exodus 20:13 does not refer to life as such, but to human life alone.

The second thing that demonstrates the high value of human life is the resurrection of Jesus Christ. It is a fact, established by the common rules of historical research, that Jesus of Nazareth not only died on a cross but also was raised from the dead on the third day. This fact is of utmost significance for many reasons, including this one: it shows us the extreme value God has placed on man, including his physical life.

Any honest reading of the New Testament must agree that it depicts the resurrection of Christ as something physical. Whether He received His glorified body at the time of the resurrection or later at the ascension, the fact remains that the resurrection was something that happened to Jesus' body. Unbelievers who reject this fact often try to reinterpret the resurrection as an entirely spiritual or psychological event. Some say it was nothing more than the rise of faith in the disciples' hearts. Others say it was just the spirit or attitude of Jesus continuing to live in His followers. Others say it was a parapsychological event: they say the actual spirit of Jesus left His body behind in the grave and entered the ethereal realm, whence it really appeared to the disciples a few times shortly thereafter.

Such views as these deny the plain testimony of Scripture, however. Jesus rose *bodily* from the dead, and He did so to effect the redemption of *our* bodies at the final resurrection. See Romans 8:23; 1 Corinthians 15:20. Through Jesus Christ God is redeeming us, body and spirit! He is saving the whole man, because the whole man is important! If physical life were insignificant (as some think), the resurrection of Christ would not have been necessary. But it *is* significant, and Jesus' bodily resurrection shows it to be so.

II. Justice and Human Life

In light of the above considerations one might think that all ethical problems related to the taking of human life can be easily solved. It might seem to be as simple as "No killing, period." But this is not the case. There is one further point that must be made before we are ready to examine the issues of life and death, namely, *physical human life is not the highest value*. As important as it is, human life is still not the most important thing.

Unfortunately many people assume that human life is the highest value, and they base many important ethical decisions on this false assumption. For some this is just a consequence of their acceptance of the theory of evolution. They view human life as the highest product of the evolutionary process; therefore it ought to have the highest respect and should be preserved at all costs. For others this notion is based on a faulty understanding of the Bible. A closer reading of the Bible will reveal the fallacies of such an idea.

In fact, the Bible teaches that a number of things, mostly intangible, are of greater value than human life. Jesus warns against absolutizing physical life when He says, "And do not fear those who kill the body, but are unable to kill the soul; but rather fear Him who is able to destroy both soul and body in hell" (Matthew 10:28). Remaining faithful to God is more important than remaining alive. Some understand Revelation 2:10 to say the same thing: "Be faithful to the end, even if you have to die" (Weymouth).

Another thing more important than life is love. Sometimes love may demand the surrender of one's life. "Greater love has no one than this, that one lay down his life for his friends" (John 15:13). See Romans 5:6-8.

One other value that may at times take precedence over life is *justice*. Even though it is never pleasant, there are times when justice can be served only by the taking of a human life. The best example of this is in the very nature of God, where justice and love are co-equal attributes. In the final judgment God's justice will require that unbelieving sinners forfeit not only their bodies but their souls as well in the eternal destruction of the lake of fire (Matthew 10:28; Revelation 20:15). Many times in His interaction with sinners upon this earth, God has pronounced the death sentence as a matter of justice. Somtimes He carried out the sentence himself (see Acts 5:1-11); sometimes He appointed others to carry it out (see Exodus 32:25-28).

At this point we should recall what we have already learned concerning God's delegation of authority to civil government, and government's purpose of seeing that justice prevails, including retributive justice. *Civil government, when justice requires it, is authorized by God to take human life.* Human life is not an absolute value that takes precedence even over justice. We will see later how this is applied to such subjects as war and capital punishment.

Now let us return to the sixth Commandment (Exodus 20:13). Many have quoted this in the translation "Thou shalt not kill" and have assumed that this is an absolute prohibition against the taking of any human life under any circumstances whatever. Unfortunately this impression may be received because of an imprecise translation of this particular verse, but anyone who examines the immediate context of the law of Moses and the total context of Scripture will see that this is false thinking.

The Hebrew word used in Exodus 20:13 is *ratzach*, which means "murder" or "kill unlawfully." When the Greek New Testament quotes the sixth Commandment, it uses the word *phoneuo*, which also means "murder." Many modern translations render Exodus 20:13 "You shall not murder." This is clearly the meaning, since the

Mosaic code itself mandated the taking of the lives of those guilty of a number of offenses, including murder! See Exodus 21:12-17.

In case there are some who think this conclusion is too harsh or that it is contrary to the nature of our loving God and our redeeming Christ, we look once more at the great life-affirming event of the resurrection of Jesus. This event is definitely a guarantee of *life* to those who know the Lord aright. But let there be no mistake: this same event of the resurrection is a guarantee of *justice* to be meted out on the Judgment Day to those who reject him. Acts 17:31 says, "He has fixed a day in which He will judge the world in righteousness through a Man whom He has appointed, having furnished proof to all men by raising Him from the dead."

God is a God of life and love, but he is also a God of justice.

Capital Punishment

Perhaps the most serious ethical problems are those that are literally matters of life or death, such as capital punishment, war, abortion, and euthanasia. Unfortunately they also tend to be the very issues over which there is the most intense disagreement. Still more unfortunate is the fact that the strongest disagreement often occurs among those who believe the Bible and accept its authority.

This is especially true of capital punishment. There are sincere Bible-believers on both sides of this issue, all claiming Biblical support. It is obviously not an easy subject to resolve, but I believe that a careful study of the relevant teachings and principles of Scripture will give a clear answer. In my judgment capital punishment *is* consistent with the teaching of both the Old Testament and the New Testament, and may even be mandated by it.

Some Christians would prefer not to think about such controversial topics, but this is not a responsible attitude. If the church is going to live up to her role as the conscience of society, we need to know how to speak out on capital punishment and other issues. Besides, any one of us may someday be on a jury dealing with a capital case. Some may be judges; some may be legislators who have to make laws on the subject. Most of us can vote for such legislators and judges; we need to know how to vote. We can do none of these properly unless we know what the Bible says about the capital punishment.

I. The Sanctity of Life

As we have already seen, God has protected human life through the sixth Commandment. Some think that this in itself rules out capital punishment. In any demonstration against capital punishment, someone will usually carry a picket sign saying, "Thou shalt not kill"—as if that settles the question. An article in *Christian Standard* a few years ago put it this way: "For exactly the same reason that it was wrong for a man to murder, it is wrong for him to *be* killed in the name of the law."

As was pointed out in the last chapter, this is a misunderstanding of the sixth Commandment, which reads literally, "You shall not murder." This commandment *does* establish the principle of the sanctity of life, but it is wrong to think that this prohibits capital punishment. In fact, the principle of the sanctity of human life is the very thing that establishes the *propriety* of the death penalty.

This is seen in God's earliest revelation on the subject, Genesis 9:5, 6. It says, "And surely I will require your lifeblood; from every beast I will require it. And from every man, from every man's brother I will require the life of man. Whoever sheds man's blood, by man his blood shall be shed, for in the image of God He made man."

This is why murder is so heinous: the murderer destroys the life of a creature *made in God's image*. Human life is thus so sacred that whoever murders another person forfeits his own right to live; this is the just punishment for his awful crime. A lesser punishment for murder is less than just.

II. The Purpose of Government

Some will agree with the above reasoning if *God himself* is the one who exacts the penalty, as when He destroyed Sodom and Gomorrah (Genesis 19:24), and Ananias and Sapphira (Acts 5:1-11). After all, God is the Creator and Lord of life; if *He* wants to do this, who can object? But surely, it is argued, *man* cannot presume to take human life; this is the prerogative of God alone.

One writer for *Christian Standard* expressed this view some years ago: "There is one irrefutable reason against capital punishment. Man cannot give life; therefore, he should not take it away. God says, 'Vengeance belongeth unto me; I will recompense, saith the Lord' (Romans 12:19, A.S.V.)."

This line of reasoning overlooks a very important principle already discussed in previous chapters, namely, the principle of *delegated authority*. The very institution of government is grounded upon this concept. To be sure, God alone is the Lord of life and death. But God has appointed civil government to act as His representative (His "minister") in this very matter of vengeance, as Romans 13:4 says. He has appointed civil rulers as His instrument for punishing evildoers (1 Peter 2:14). This is a major part of justice, which is the purpose of government.

God's first word on capital punishment makes this clear enough: "Whoever sheds man's blood, *by man* his blood shall be shed" (Genesis 9:6).

If anyone doubts that God has approved death as the appropriate punishment for certain crimes, or that He has appointed human government to carry out the death sentence, he needs only to examine the law of Moses. This law was revealed by God and embodies His will for His people between the time of Moses and the beginning of the church. It included both broad moral principles and a detailed criminal code. Included in the latter were a number of crimes for which death was the specified penalty. A partial list of these is as follows:

1. Murder—Exodus 21:12-14; Numbers 35:30.
2. Kidnapping—Exodus 21:16; Deuteronomy 24:7.
3. Adultery—Leviticus 20:10; Deuteronomy 22:22-24.
4. Incest—Leviticus 20:11, 12, 14.
5. Homosexual acts—Leviticus 20:13.
6. Striking or cursing a parent—Exodus 21:15, 17.
7. Rebelling against parents—Deuteronomy 21:18-21.
8. Witchcraft and spiritism—Exodus 22:18; Leviticus 20:27.
9. Cursing God—Leviticus 24:10-16.
10. Trying to lead people to serve false gods—Deuteronomy 13:1-11; 18:20.

In all these cases and more, God declared that the punishment should be death, and He expected this punishment to be carried out under the supervision of the local authorities. This shows that capital punishment is not inherently wrong, and it shows that civil government is the divinely authorized means for carrying it out.

III. The Purpose of Punishment

Some will agree that God has appointed civil rulers to punish evildoers (1 Peter 2:14), but they believe that capital punishment cannot be included because it is contrary to the very purpose of punishment. This raises an important question, namely, what *is* the purpose for punishing criminals?

Some of the most common concepts of punishment today fall into the category that C. S. Lewis calls "The Humanitarian Theory of Punishment" (*God in the Dock,* Eerdmans 1970, pp. 287-300.) These are the views that say punishment should be applied only for humane or even merciful reasons. Among these are the ideas that punishment should serve to deter further crime and that it should rehabilitate the criminal. Absent from this approach is the view that punishment should be exacted simply because the criminal *deserves* it, i.e., as retribution. This is considered to be a barbaric and archaic theory of punishment.

Capital punishment is hardly rehabilitative, and many argue that it fails as a deterrent. Thus it must be basically an act of revenge or retribution, which on the "humanitarian" theory is ruled out.

From the Biblical perspective the humanitarian approach is inadequate. It fails basically because it does not recognize that the purpose of government is *justice,* not mercy. The essence of justice is to see that each one gets what he deserves, whether it be praise for good or punishment for evil. Thus the Biblical rationale for punishing criminals is retribution: they are punished because they deserve it. The civil ruler is "an avenger who brings wrath upon the one who practices evil" (Romans 13:4).

God laid down this principle of retributive justice in the law of Moses when He gave the "eye for an eye" rule to guide civil judges in meting out proper penalties. See Exodus 21:23-25; Leviticus 24:19, 20; and Deuteronomy 19:21.

That retribution is the basic reason for punishment is seen most vividly in the fact of *Hell*. This final penalty for sinners is certainly not rehabilitative, and it will not deter further sin. Its purpose is simply to give the sinner what he deserves. Such action is not contrary to or unworthy of the nature of God. Justice and wrath are an important part of His nature, one we dare not overlook, "for our God is a consuming fire" (Hebrews 12:29).

The death penalty is thus perfectly consistent with the purpose of punishment as taught in Scripture. It is openly and without apology an act of retribution, a penalty exacted just because the wrongdoer deserves it.

It should be noted, however, that deterrence is an equally valid end to be sought in the punishment of crime. Whether a particular penalty actually deters further crime is in one sense irrelevant, since it is being applied for retribution. But the very knowledge that a certain crime *will* be punished by a certain penalty *should* deter others from doing it.

This is, in fact, the way in which civil government accomplishes its ultimate end of preserving the peace. It will be remembered that the government achieves this aim through *fear*. It protects the law-abiding by instilling fear into the hearts of potential lawbreakers. How does it do this? By the swift and just punishment of those who do break the law. When one sees the penalty being applied, he will think twice before committing his unlawful deed. As Romans 13:3, 4 says, rulers are a cause of fear for evil behavior. So, "if you do what is evil, be afraid; for it does not bear the sword for nothing."

The death penalty specifically is intended to act as a deterrent. Some believe that Paul's reference to the sword in Romans 13:4 is an allusion to the government's authority to impose capital punishment. Whether this is so or not, the death penalty's purpose as a deterrent is clear in some of the more detailed rules regarding capital crimes in the Mosaic law.

For instance, Deuteronomy 21:18 gives this sobering instruction: "If any man has a stubborn and rebellious son who will not obey his father or his mother," they shall seize him and deliver him over to the elders of his city. "Then all the men of his city shall stone him to death; so shall you remove the evil from your midst, *and all Israel shall hear of it and fear.*" See Deuteronomy 17:12, 13; 19:15-21.

Thus capital punishment, like any other civil punishment, should and will be a deterrent if justly, swiftly, and openly applied. To those who argue that it is in fact *not* an effective deterrent we reply as follows: (1) statistical studies on this question can never be conclusive; (2) since retribution is the main purpose of punishment, it should be applied anyway even if it does not deter others; (3) if it is ineffective as a deterrent, this is due to the flaws in our system of justice. Regarding this last point, the Bible teaches that if a penalty is not applied swiftly, it will not have its intended deterrent effect. Ecclesiastes 8:11 says, "Because the sentence against an evil deed is not executed quickly, therefore the hearts of the sons of men among them are given fully to do evil." This is a frighteningly accurate description of our judicial system. If capital punishment is in fact not a deterrent, the remedy is not to abandon the punishment but to apply it more surely and swiftly.

In summary, the Bible shows that the main purpose of punishment is retribution, and that the intended secondary effect is deterrence. Capital punishment is perfectly consistent with this view.

IV. The Coming of Jesus

Now we come to the most serious objection to capital punishment as many Bible-believers see it. Their point is that this practice was accepted in the Old Testament age, since the ethical standards were lower then; but things are different in the New Testament age. When Jesus came, He brought a newer and higher ethic: love your neighbor, love your enemy, turn the other cheek. By both His teaching and His example, as some see it, Jesus put an end to all prior permission to take human life. The law of *love* is now supreme, and this rules out *all* killing. See Matthew 5:38-48; Romans 12:17-21; John 13:34, 35.

This is a well-meaning and serious objection, but it is completely misguided. It is based on a false understanding of the purpose, life, and teachings of Jesus. It assumes that one of Christ's main purposes for coming was to reveal and model a higher ethical ideal. This is definitely not the case.

Revelation was not the main purpose of the incarnation; *redemption* was. The teachings revealed by Christ during His ministry were secondary, even incidental, to His work as high priest and Redeemer.

The *life* of Jesus was not necessary to provide us with an ethical model, nor was it intended to do so in all respects. In a general sense we "follow in His steps" (1 Peter 2:21), but we cannot do so in all details, for His purpose and work were unique.

Likewise the *teaching* of Christ was never intended to provide a complete ethical system. He taught what was necessary for His mission, but left the bulk of His teaching to the apostles through the inspiration of the Spirit (John 16:12-15). The writings of Paul, John, and others complement and complete the "red-letter" sections of the Gospels.

When we understand that Christ's coming was not primarily to reveal but to redeem, then we can better understand that Jesus did *not* introduce a new system of ethics. His general ethical teaching, especially as it relates to love, justice, and government, is not a newer and higher moral standard. Jesus taught what always had been and what continues to be God's will on these matters. See Matthew 5:17-20.

It is absolutely essential to see this point, especially since many base their objection to capital punishment on a supposed revolution in ethics wrought by Jesus.

Let us note especially that Christ's teaching in Matthew 5:38-48 and His love ethic in general are *nothing new*. "Love your neighbor" and "turn the other cheek" has *always* been God's rule for the individual's personal relationships with others. Neighbor-love has always forbidden the spirit of vengeance. Leviticus 19:18 taught it clearly: "You shall not take vengeance, nor bear any grudge against the sons of your people, but you shall love your neighbor as yourself; I am the Lord."

Likewise Jesus' reference to "an eye for an eye" in Matthew 5:38 was not intended to do away with this principle of justice, as some think. The references to Old Testament teaching in Matthew 5 were not necessarily intended to put aside the teachings themselves, but only the current false interpretations and applications of them. (See verses 21, 27, for example.) In Jesus' day the "eye for an eye" principle was being used to justify personal revenge, whereas it was originally intended for use only by civil magistrates in deciding just punishments. Personal revenge was forbidden. Jesus was simply calling people back to the original teaching.

Conclusive proof that Christ was not setting aside the principle of justice as the standard for government is seen in Romans 12:17—13:4. Here this very principle is taught *side by side* with the admonition to "resist not evil." One applies to the official activities of governments; the other applies to personal relationships between individuals. *Both are still valid today*. THIS IS A KEY POINT.

It is crucial to study the Romans 12—13 passage without stopping at the chapter division. In 12:19 Paul says, "Never take your own revenge, beloved, but leave room for the WRATH of God, for it is written, 'VENGEANCE is Mine, I will repay, says the Lord.' " Those who wrongly think this refers only to the final judgment must read on into chapter 13, especially verse 4: the *civil ruler* is "an AVENGER who brings WRATH upon the one who practices evil."

This is why we are forbidden to take personal revenge: because God has set up His own system for bringing His own wrath and vengeance upon evildoers! That capital punishment is still a part of that system is seen in Paul's affirmation of it in Acts 25:11. Here he is falsely accused by the Jews and under arrest by Rome. He declares, "If then I am a wrongdoer, and have committed anything *worthy of death, I do not refuse to die*." (Of course he was innocent, so he appealed to Caesar.)

The conclusion is that the coming of Jesus did not change the purpose of government, nor did it introduce a higher ethic for individuals. Civil authorities are still responsible for maintaining justice and executing wrath on evildoers, and personal vengeance is still wrong.

V. Miscellaneous Objections

Some miscellaneous objections to the death penalty remain. A few are based on further misunderstanding of Scripture. For instance, why didn't Jesus demand the death penalty for the woman caught in adultery, as the law of Moses required? (John 8:1-11). Because He knew those who brought her to Him were only trying to trap him. Their hypocrisy was evident in the fact that they did not bring the *man* to Jesus too, since they caught them in "the very act."

Other objections are theoretical and must be addressed to God himself. If the objections are valid, then God was wrong for introducing capital punishment in the first place. For instance, it is said that capital punishment is wrong because it rules out the possibility for repentance. We reply that a person who does something "worthy of death" forfeits his right to any further opportunities. Also, this did not stop God from the judicial exercise of His wrath on the many occasions when He brought death upon the guilty (e.g., Sodom and Gomorrah).

Another objection is that capital punishment is wrong because it cannot be administered fairly; at times even an innocent person might be killed. True, *perfect* administration may not be possible, but it is not necessary if certain Biblical safeguards are followed. For instance, *eyewitness* testimony, always by *more* than one witness, was required for conviction under the Mosaic code (Deuteronomy 17:6; 19:15). Also the witnesses were motivated to be very careful and truthful: false testimony brought upon the perjurer the *same penalty* he sought to inflict upon the innocent party through his perjury (Deuteronomy 19:16, 19). Besides, this is not an argument against capital punishment as such, but against poor administration of it.

Others say murderers (or criminals as such) are sick and should be cured, not killed. True, *all* sin is the result of a spiritual sickness of the heart (Jeremiah 17:9), but this releases the sinner neither from moral responsibility nor from liability for punishment. Otherwise there would be no Hell.

In conclusion we must say that a heavy responsibility lies upon lawmakers and law-enforcers in this matter of capital punishment. Since the Mosaic code was intended only for Old Testament Israel, we do not follow its details on this subject. Each state must determine what, in its time and circumstances, is a crime "worthy of death." It must also see that the penalty is carried out justly and quickly.

There is little doubt that capital punishment has been ordained and sanctioned by God. The sobering question that must be faced now is this: if God has ordained it, is it wrong *not* to use it?

War

An escaped convict is trying to break into your house. As he tries the doors and windows, you call the police. "Hurry!" you say. Just as the convict has succeeded in breaking the lock on your front door, the police arrive and order him to stop. He turns and fires a gun at them. The police return the fire and the convict slumps over, dead.

Your missionary compound has been attacked by a group of terrorist guerrillas. They do not intend to take prisoners. You finally make radio contact with the local government headquarters. Two helicopter gunships arrive just as a final attack is being launched on the compound. The terrorists open fire on the helicopters, but the government forces reply with several rockets. A number of guerrillas are killed, and the rest flee. You and your missionary personnel are safe.

Your nation is invaded by the armed forces of a neighboring anti-God, anti-freedom dictator-state. If they succeed in their attempt to take over your country, the women will be violated, possessions pillaged, and all religion and religious believers eradicated. Your government is ready, however, and a defensive counter-attack is begun. After much fierce fighting, the invading troops are defeated and driven out.

Try to imagine yourself actually involved in the series of situations just described. What would be your reaction as each episode unfolds? Would you be grateful to the policemen? Would you be glad they had guns with them when they answered your call? Would you thank God that the helicopters arrived in time? Would you be glad that your troops were able to repulse the invading army? Would you praise your government for being prepared for such a war?

The basic question in each case is the ethical one: was the action taken by the civil authorities moral or immoral? A few people would say that the government acted wrongly each time. They believe that the use of force is *always* evil, and that even the policemen in the first episode were doing wrong. (This is an extreme form of pacifism.)

A fair number of people, including many who are attempting to follow Biblical teaching, would conclude that what the policemen did in the first case was acceptable, and they may approve of even the second incident. The third example, however, they would condemn as immoral: that's *war,* and war is wrong. (This is a more common form of pacifism.)

Finally there are many people, also including many Bible-believers, who would say that the government was acting properly, morally, and in accord with its God-ordained responsibility in all three cases. They maintain that there is no real difference in kind between the defensive war in the third illustration and the more limited police action in the other two examples. It would seem that the government is doing exactly the same kind of thing in each case, so that if one is right, all are right.

This last position seems to me to be the correct one, the one supported by Biblical teaching. As presented and defended here, it is known as the "just war" position. It says that certain circumstances not only justify but even require a government's going to war.

I. War and Justice

The starting point in any consideration of the morality of warfare is the Bible's teaching concerning the purpose of government, which we have already discussed. As we saw, the main task of government is to promote, preserve, and enforce *justice,* which is "the just rendering to each man of his due" (as Aristotle defined it).

We also saw that justice has two major aspects. One is *distributive* justice, which includes protecting the rights of the innocent, such as the right to live and the right to be free from oppression (1 Timothy 2:1-4). The other is *retributive* justice, which is the punishing of those who deserve it because of their violations of the rights of others.

Since the big ethical issue relating to war is the taking of human life, we may ask first of all whether such killing is permissible as an act of retributive justice. The answer is *yes,* as can be seen in the following comparison.

We have seen that murder is wrong because it is the taking of innocent life, but capital punishment is right as just retribution against a murderer. Most wars follow this pattern. When one nation launches an attack against another, bent on conquest, pillage, and destruction, it incurs guilt in the same way that a murderer does, only on a much larger scale. Individual soldiers participating in the act of aggression share in this guilt, and thus become liable to death in the interests of retributive justice. Thus it is morally right for an attacked nation, in the process of defending itself, to kill the guilty aggressors. It is the moral equivalent of capital punishment.

The main consideration in the issue of warfare is not retributive but *distributive* justice, which in the final analysis is the ultimate purpose of government. A God-fearing government will do its best to provide its citizens with a just, free, and peaceable environment. It will protect its people from acts of injustice, whether committed by individuals or by aggressor nations. This leads us to ask whether this responsibility gives a government the right to engage in warfare and killing as a means of protecting its citizens. The answer is *yes:* it is a matter not only of justice, but also of *love*.

It is often thought that the love-ethic rules out any sort of participation in war. After all, one should love his enemies; so how can he shoot them? The fact is, however, that this does not take into account another facet of love, namely, our love for the innocent citizens who themselves stand to be enslaved or killed by an attacking army. *What is love's responsibility to them?* In general we can say that love requires us to seek distributive justice for the innocent; and specifically love requires us to defend their rights in the case of aggressive attack, even to the point of armed defense, and even if it involves killing the guilty aggressors. Love's responsibility to protect the innocent must prevail in this case.

Thus we conclude that a defensive war is justified by both aspects of justice, and even by love itself. Pacifism—"peace at any price"—is not a Biblical position. As has been explained, physical human life is not the highest value. Refusing to take human life even where love and justice demand it is a distortion of proper values.

II. The Just War

The kind of thinking outlined above has led to the concept of the "just war" (i.e., a *justified* war). This is one of the major viewpoints accepted as Biblical throughout most of Christian history, and I believe it is the correct one.

The term *just war* does not refer to war as such or to any war considered in its totality. It refers rather to only one side of any given war, namely, the side that is merely trying to defend itself against attack. The aggressor's side is *not* considered to be just. Its invasion, with murder as well as robbery, is a crime that deserves punishment, even capital punishment.

A just war is defined not only in terms of its goal (namely, defense), but also in terms of the means by which this goal is sought. Even where a nation's cause is just, it has been determined that certain ways of conducting warfare are unjust.

By carefully considering both the means and the end of combat, many Christian and secular thinkers have come to general agreement as to what constitutes just warfare. The following is a listing of its characteristics as compiled by Arthur F. Holmes. (See the book edited by him, *War and Christian Ethics,* Baker Book House, pp. 4, 5.)

1. The just war must have a *just cause*. The only legitimate cause is self-defense. (Some would argue that a preventive first strike against a nation planning an imminent attack falls in the category of self-defense. An example of this would be Israel's action in the Six Days' War of 1967.)

2. The just war must have a *just intent*. That is, it must be seeking only to restore peace, and not to inflict destruction and revenge upon the enemy.

3. The just war must be the *last resort*. The government should have tried other means, such as negotiation and compromise, to ward off aggression.

4. The just war must be *lawfully declared*. Only the lawfully-established government may make the decision to take up arms. Individuals and private militia groups do not have this right.

5. The just war must respect the *immunity of noncombatants*. Only those who are actively fighting or actively supporting the fighting in behalf of an aggressor nation are legitimate "targets" in the cause of self-defense. Every precaution must be taken to spare innocent civilians. Indiscriminate bombing and terrorist acts are thus ruled out.

The advent of nuclear weapons makes it very difficult to abide by this condition for just warfare. The destructive capacity of hydrogen bombs, for instance, makes it virtually impossible to use them without killing large numbers of non-combatants. Thus some would argue that the "just war" theory is inapplicable in the nuclear age; therefore our only alternative is to become pacifists. Others argue that even nuclear weapons may be used justly if directed against tactical targets and not cities with their civilian populations.

Needless to say, this is a very difficult question. It is no doubt the most problematic aspect of the just war concept today.

6. The just war must have *limited objectives,* in accord with its limited intent. For instance, it need not press for unconditional surrender, and it need not destroy the enemy's economy.

7. The just war must be fought with *limited means*. No greater force should be used than is necessary to restore peace.

It is fairly easy to list these conditions for just warfare; being able to abide by them in an actual combat situation is much more difficult indeed. Nevertheless, if a nation commits itself to military involvement only under these conditions, and sincerely attempts to apply them as conscientiously as possible, it is doing right in God's sight.

We should add that if this is true, then defense preparations are a necessary and legitimate part of government spending. The degree of preparation and the amount spent will depend upon the nature of the danger of being attacked. Where the threat of attack and conquest by a powerful nation is strong, the preparations for defense must be extensive, in order to deter the enemy. (This is, of course, the primary purpose of a country's military capability: not to fight a war, but to cause a potential aggressor to *fear* the consequences of attack. This is in perfect accord with Romans 13:1-4.)

III. War and The Christian

Even when it is acknowledged that a government has the right to fight a defensive war, an important question still remains. Is it right for a *Christian* to participate in such a war? Or is the Christian under a higher, different standard, which rules out his involvement in war of *any* kind? Some take this latter position, arguing that wars may sometimes be a necessary evil but that Christians can never take part in them. This must be left up to the sinners in government service.

I believe that this is faulty thinking. God's standards of right and wrong are the same for everybody. If Jesus did bring a higher standard, it applies to everyone alike, even though Christians may be the only ones to acknowledge it. If war is always wrong, it is just as wrong for unbelievers as it is for Christians. But if war is sometimes justified, it is right for Christians to participate in it the same as sinners.

The question must be asked again, however, whether Jesus indeed *did* bring a higher ethic that rules out Christians' participating in even just wars. As we saw in the last chapter, this is not the case. Jesus did not set aside justice and introduce love as something new to take its place. He emphasized the necessity of the rule of love in personal relationships, but he left the rule of justice intact as the official standard for governmental action. (This is clear from Paul's endorsement of both in Romans 12:17—13:4.) Remember also that both are taught in the Old Testament as well as the New.

Some argue that Jesus is our supreme example, and that it is impossible to imagine Jesus with a gun in his hand, much less firing it at another human being. We say two things in reply. First, to whatever extent the life of Jesus is an example for us, it is an example in the area of person-to-person relationships, not governmental action. Jesus was not a civil ruler and did not intend to be a role model for human governments.

Second, those who think the example of Jesus is exclusively one of non-violence, self-sacrifice, and love are forgetting what the Bible says about His *second* coming. Those who can't imagine the meek Jesus with a gun in His hand will have a terrible time with such passages as 2 Thessalonians 1:6-9; Revelation 6:16, 17; and Revelation 19:11-16. Here His justice, wrath, and vengeance are displayed in all their frightening reality as they are unleashed against those who deserve them.

Surely God is love, but He is also a consuming fire. Jesus is the epitome of love, but He is also the essence of justice. Each has its place, and each has its priorities. Love, meekness, and non-resistance shape our personal relationships with other individuals (Matthew 5:38-48; Romans 12:17-21). However, the principle of justice shapes our actions insofar as we are officially representing our government, whether it be as a policeman, judge, or soldier.

This brings us to the crucial question: is it really possible for a member of Christ's kingdom to carry out the functions of the state? Can a Christian effectively operate in both spheres at the same time?

Some think the sphere of God's kingdom and the sphere of civil government are mutually exclusive, and that a person cannot consistently function in both at the same time. They consider the state to be something evil, "the realm ruled by principalities and powers against which the children of the kingdom wrestle," as one writer put it. Thus when a person becomes a Christian, he can enter the kingdom of God only by separating himself from the state. One must choose to obey one or the other; he cannot do both. Particularly, a Christian cannot engage in war under any circumstances. If this is to be done at all, it must be left up to the "bad guys" who function as the state.

Another view (the *Biblical* view, I believe) is that though the church and state are different and perform different functions, they do not conflict with one another but *complement* each other. Certainly the civil government is engaged in activities not assigned to the church, but that is by God's design. Its functions may not be pleasant, but they are not evil; its purposes and duties are God-appointed and are just as valid and righteous as the work of the church. See Romans 13:1-4 again.

Thus a Christian can function consistently in both spheres at the same time. In his personal relationships he acts in love toward others as God has always required individuals to do. But if he also happens to play a role in civil government, he acts in accord with its God-ordained purposes when carrying out his official duties. *There is no contradiction here.* A Christian can participate in any legitimate function of government, even warfare if it is just, without violating God's will for personal conduct.

The key word, of course, is *legitimate*. We must always sit in judgment upon the activities of our government, fully supporting it when it is right but refusing to support it when it is wrong. Thus if a government embarks upon a course of action contrary to God's purposes, such as an unjust war, then a Christian must *refuse* to participate—and suffer the consequences. But if the sad occasion arises where a government must declare war in order to defend its people's life and freedoms, we must support that effort, responding to a draft call where given. This is called selective conscientious objection. It is the only position truly consistent with the "just war" concept.

We conclude that pacifism as such is not supported by Biblical teaching. However, the conscience of a pacifist, though misinformed, must be respected.

Abortion

Abortion is the most frequently performed operation in the United States. One and one-half million abortions were performed here in 1980; about one-third of all pregnancies ended in abortions.

These facts were reported by George F. Will in a recent column in *Newsweek* (June 22, 1981; page 92). They illustrate the magnitude of the abortion problem, and they underscore how important it is for Christians to be properly informed on the subject. In this chapter we shall attempt to present the basic information, particularly from Scripture, that will enable us to come to firm conclusions about the matter.

I. The Question of Personhood

In chapter 5 we discussed the unique nature of human beings as creatures made in God's image. We are qualitatively different from all other earthly life. Unlike animals, we are *spirit* as well as body.

As a result, only human beings are *persons*. Personhood is part of the very essence of spiritual existence. All spiritual beings are personal. God is spirit (John 4:24); therefore God is personal. We are spirit; therefore we are persons. This is the very essence of being made in God's image.

The most important implication of personhood is this: we have an innate capacity for a personal relationship with God. We are spiritually equipped to know God and to enter into communion with Him. This inherent capacity is what makes human life *human* and different from all other life.

It should be emphasized that this quality of personhood belongs to a one-week-old baby just the same as it does to a thirty-year-old man. The baby has not yet developed a conscious relationship with God, but he has the *capacity* for it. He is not qualitatively different from the adult. (As we shall see, this also applies to the one-week-old fetus.)

Because human life is uniquely in God's image, God has placed it under the special protection of the sixth Commandment: "You shall not murder" (Exodus 20:13). As we have seen, God allows the taking of human life in the interests of justice, but all other deliberate killing of another human being is MURDER.

Here is the basic Biblical rationale for opposing abortion. Abortion is the deliberate killing of an innocent human being; therefore it is *murder* and stands condemned by the sixth Commandment.

Some would argue that it is inconsistent to defend capital punishment and oppose abortion at the same time. However, they fail to see the fundamental difference between innocent life and guilty life. Capital punishment involves only the guilty; it is deserved punishment; and it can be administered only by civil authorities as a judicial act. Abortion, on the other hand, is the killing of an *innocent* person without even a trial. Surely this distinction is obvious to all.

"But wait just a minute," replies the abortion advocate. "This is just the point at stake. Whoever said the unborn infant is a person?" Indeed, this *is* the crucial issue in the whole abortion debate: *Is the unborn child a person?*

This question is all the more critical in view of the 1973 Supreme Court decision, which in effect legalized abortion at any stage of pregnancy. The fourteenth amendment to our Constitution guarantees the right to life for every U.S. citizen in these words: "Nor shall any State deprive any person of life, liberty, or property, without due process of law: nor deny to any person within its jurisdiction the equal protection of the laws." The Supreme Court, however, decreed that this *does not apply* to unborn children, since the unborn are not persons! Here are its exact words: "The word 'person,' as used in the Fourteenth Amendment, does not include the unborn" *(Roe v. Wade Decision,* page 43).

With these words the Court opened the floodgates of death for nearly ten million babies thus far. It decreed that a woman may have an abortion *for any reason* through approximately the first two-thirds of her pregnancy. It further decreed that she may have an abortion at any time thereafter if her life or health is at stake. The latter is taken to include mental and emotional health, and this is interpreted in such a broad fashion that it includes any woman who is upset at the prospect of having her baby. Thus, thanks to the Supreme Court, any woman who really wants an abortion can legally have one at *any time*. State legislatures no longer have the power to forbid it by law.

We must remember this, however: *legal* is not necessarily the same as *moral*. The mere fact that something is legal doesn't mean it is right. This, we conclude, is exactly the case with abortion. Contrary to the Court's decision, we believe the unborn *are* persons, and that their right to life is protected not only by the fourteenth amendment but also by God's commandment, "You shall not murder."

II. Proof of Personhood

When does human life begin? When does the fetus receive its soul? At what point does the developing baby become a person? No matter how the question is asked, the answer is the same: *at conception*. There is absolutely no basis for assuming otherwise. The selection of any other point of time (e.g., implantation, "quickening," viability, or birth) is purely arbitrary.

There are two main lines of evidence for the personhood of the unborn child. One is the witness of Scripture; the other is the testimony of medical science.

The Biblical witness is indirect but convincing. The Bible nowhere specifically discusses the personhood of the unborn; it simply assumes it. It refers to children in the womb as persons important to God and as individuals in whom God is personally interested. The most significant of such references is Psalm 139:13-16, which reads,

> For Thou didst form my inward parts;
> Thou didst weave me in my mother's womb.
> I will give thanks to Thee, for I am fearfully
>   and wonderfully made;
> Wonderful are Thy works,
> And my soul knows it very well.
> My frame was not hidden from Thee,
> When I was made in secret,
> And skillfully wrought in the depths of the earth.
> Thine eyes have seen my unformed substance;
> And in Thy book they were all written,
> The days that were ordained for me,
> When as yet there was not one of them.

Here David describes his prenatal existence in personal terms ("me," "my") and as the object of God's care and attention. As one writer says, "It seems that the psalmist did not think of his humanity as uniquely tied to the moment of birth."

Other individuals whose personal identity is affirmed while they were yet in the womb are Jeremiah (Jeremiah 1:5), Paul (Galatians 1:15), John the Baptist (Luke 1:15, 36, 41-44), and Jesus himself (Luke 1:41-44). Luke's reference to John and Jesus is especially important, since Jesus was just newly-conceived at the time. Nevertheless Elizabeth refers to Him as "my Lord"! Also notable is the Greek word used to describe John in Verses 41 and 44, namely, *brephos* ("baby"). This word is used in the New Testament and elsewhere to refer to infants whether born or unborn. This suggests that the child does not enter some new level of life at birth; he is just as much a baby—a person—before birth as after.

Another relevant Biblical passage is Galatians 5:20, which condemns as a "deed of the flesh" the practice of sorcery or witchcraft. The word here is *pharmakeia*, which actually means "witchdoctoring by using drugs" (compare our word *pharmacy*). One of the most common reasons why women visited such "medicine men" in ancient times was to obtain a drug to induce abortion. (See John T. Noonan, Jr., *The Morality of Abortion*, Harvard University Press, pp. 8-10.)

Two passages of Scripture are sometimes misused in an effort to justify abortion. One is Genesis 2:7, which in the King James Version reads: "And the Lord God formed man of the dust of the ground, and breathed into his nostrils the breath of life; and man became a living soul." The contention is that Adam did not receive his "soul" until he began to breathe; therefore babies do not have souls until they are born and begin to breathe. Thus it is all right to have an abortion.

This is a totally false reading of Genesis 2:7. The word *soul* as used here does not refer to the spiritual nature of Adam at all. It is used in the broader sense of "being." It simply means that Adam became a *living being*, i.e., he became alive, at the moment God breathed into him. The very same Hebrew expresssion, "living being" or "living creature," is used of animals in Genesis 1:20, 21, 24. Even if Genesis 2:7 *did* refer to Adam's soul (which it does not), this would not tell us anything about when babies receive their souls. After all, babies do not come into existence in the same way as Adam. They certainly are alive before they begin to breathe.

The other passage sometimes misused to justify abortion is Exodus 21:22-25, which tells what punishment to apply if brawling men strike a pregnant woman. Because of an unfortunate yet persistent mistranslation this passage is often understood as follows: (1) If there is merely a "miscarriage, yet . . . no further injury," the guilty party shall pay a simple fine. (2) But if there is further injury, i.e., to the mother herself, then the rule of "life for life, eye for eye" shall apply. The inference is then drawn that the life of the fetus is less important than the life of the mother; therefore abortion is allowed.

This is a false reading of the passage. Exodus 21:22 does not say "miscarriage," though this word occurs in many translations. Nor does it speak of *further* injury: this word is *added* by the translators. It says literally, "If her children come out, yet there is no harm"—that is, if there is merely a premature birth—then a fine is imposed. Verse 23 says, "But if there be harm," then the "life for life" rule applies. It does *not* distinguish between harm to the mother and harm to the baby. Harm to *either* is punishable in the same way. The baby is *not* accorded inferior status.

The Bible thus speaks of unborn life in the same way as post-natal life. There is no hint that a special change occurs at some point such as birth. From its beginning the baby is human life, a human person. What else *could* it be? It is qualitatively distinct from all other life. Once its existence begins, it can never be any more or less human. There is no magic line which, when crossed, transforms the baby into a person. We do not *acquire* personhood; it is ours by nature.

The testimony of medical science supports this view in every way. Research within the last two or three decades has given us quite thorough details of fetal development. We know what the baby is like at every stage of growth. The picture is one of an unbroken continuum from conception onward.

At fertilization the single cell is unique and distinct, with its own chromosomal and genetic structure. It is *not* a part of the mother's body. The remarkable thing is that this single cell contains *everything* that the full-grown adult will be. It only needs time and nourishment to unfold and grow. Nothing new will be added. The one-celled person is not qualitatively different from what he will be at twenty-five years of age.

Within twenty-one days the baby's backbone, spinal cord, and nervous system are forming. A small heart is present and beating.

At one month arms and legs are present. There is a head with rudimentary eyes, ears, mouth, and brain. The digestive system has begun. The baby is still only one-fourth of an inch long, but he is ten thousand times larger than when he began.

At two months the baby is fully formed. He reacts to stimuli such as tickling. He will try to grasp a tiny instrument with his tiny hand. He "swims" or moves about in the amniotic fluid. He has fingerprints.

By the end of the third month, as one observer notes, "he can kick his legs, turn his feet, curl and fan his toes, make a fist, move his thumb, bend his wrist, turn his head, squint, frown, open his mouth," swallow, and breathe (fluid, or course). Fingernails are forming.

Is this a human being, a person? Of course! How could he be anything else? Understanding fetal growth from the perspective of medical research helps us to appreciate the Bible's respect for the unborn. It also shows the tragedy of the Supreme Court's decree that the unborn are not persons.

III. Procedures and Problems

As unpleasant as it is, we must briefly describe how abortions are done. During the first three months two methods are most common. One is called "D & C," or dilatation and curettage. In this procedure (used for other purposes, too), the abortionist inserts a sharp, curved instrument through the dilated cervix and scrapes the wall of the womb to remove the baby and its placenta. The baby is usually cut into pieces.

Also used in the early months is the suction method. Here a suction tube is inserted into the womb. When the machine is turned on, the baby and placenta, ripped into pieces, are sucked out into a jar.

In the later months of pregnancy a common method of abortion is salt-poisoning. Using a needle, the abortionist removes some amniotic fluid and replaces it with a strong salt solution. For the next hour or more the baby breathes and swallows this corroding solution, while his whole outer body is being burned raw. He dies in pain, literally poisoned. The mother goes into labor and delivers the dead baby. (Some have been born alive.)

Another method for later months is hysterotomy, or simple removal of the baby by Caesarian section. The baby is simply removed and discarded. (Here and in the last paragraph we are talking about babies weighing up to three or four pounds.)

The latest accepted method is the use of the drug prostaglandin. It simply induces labor, which causes the developing baby to be born. In early pregnancy the trauma itself usually kills the baby. In later months the baby may be born alive, but with proper neglect it will soon die anyway.

It should be noted that certain "contraceptives" actually work through the principle of abortion. They do not prevent the conception of a new person, but rather prevent the implantation of the developing person in the wall of the uterus (which usually occurs about the seventh day). The I.U.D. and the "morning-after" pill almost certainly work by this method, and more recent versions of *the* contraceptive pill (with reduced estrogen content) are likely to function this way at least part of the time. Users of these types of contraceptives must examine their hearts and consciences in light of their convictions on abortion.

If abortion at any stage is the killing of a human person—and it is, I believe—then it is *always* wrong. Are there *no* exceptions? One must, of course, apply the principle of the lesser of two evils. Is there any circumstance which would be a greater evil than the loss of the baby's life? In my judgment, only one: the loss of the mother's life. Only when continuation of the pregnancy would cause the mother's death are we justified in performing an abortion, and then with sorrow and reluctance.

Other circumstances are definitely traumatic and even tragic, but they are not a greater evil than killing an innocent baby. Rape and incest are very real horrors, but following these up with abortion only compounds the problem. An abortion can never erase the fact of a rape. If the violated woman cannot bear the prospect of raising the child, it can be surrendered for adoption. Remember: the baby is innocent. It must not be punished for the crime of its father.

Sometimes the mother-to-be has other emotional problems, but again abortion only adds to them. Abortion, it has been noted, has its own "psychological price."

Often a discovered defect in the developing baby is considered to be a just cause for abortion. (Genetic defects such as Down's Syndrome are commonly detected today, via a procedure called amniocentesis.) This is allegedly done for the baby's sake: it just would not be fair to ask him to endure such a low quality of life. Let's be honest. Are we really thinking of the baby, or of ourselves? Are we just unwilling to bear the burden? Remember: a defective baby is a *human* baby, and innocent as well. The taking of innocent human life is still murder. Besides, defects are not always handicaps. Some of the sweetest, most sensitive persons are in this category.

The final question is one of rights. Doesn't a woman have the right to privacy, i.e., the right to do what she wants with her "own body"? Maybe; maybe not. But that is not the question, because the baby is *not her body*. He is a person with his *own* rights. Whatever rights a woman has over her own body do not allow her to violate the most basic right of another human being: the right to life.

9

Euthanasia

The battle to protect innocent human lives is being fought on several fronts. Thus far most of the attention has been focused on abortion, but most agree that this is only the beginning. "Abortion has been legalized throughout Europe and in the Western hemisphere, but don't think the battle is over," says one observer. Another comments, "By making abortion-on-demand the law of the land, the Supreme Court set the stage for infanticide and euthanasia."

Euthanasia is a word taken directly from the Greek language; it means literally "an easy death" or "a good death." It usually refers to the deliberate inducement of death for a person suffering an unbearable trauma of some kind. As one definition puts it, "Euthanasia is the purposeful killing of a dependent human being, allegedly for his own good." Hence the common term *mercy killing*.

Probably no ethical problem presents us with more complexities and dilemmas than this one. We are confronted with a wide range of genetic defects, devastating diseases, and crippling accidents. Scientific advances in life-saving and life-prolonging equipment and techniques make it possible to maintain a person with almost any kind of deteriorating condition in a state of life or near-life. At the same time the person's suffering or hopelessness causes us to wonder whether death would be preferable to the mere parody of life that remains.

The ethical question is this: Is it ever right to induce or hasten the death of a person in such a situation? Sometimes the question must be put negatively: Is it ever right to decide *not* to do something that would prolong the life of a sufferer? In this chapter we will suggest some answers to these questions.

I. Bible Truth About Death

The starting point for a consideration of euthanasia is the Bible's teaching about death. Whatever conclusions are reached on this difficult subject *must* be consistent with these foundational truths of God's revelation.

The first Biblical truth is that *death is an enemy to mankind*. It is an alien intruder into the human race; it is unnatural for men to die. The Bible makes it quite clear that physical death was not God's purpose for His highest creatures. From the beginning it was a possibility, however, contingent upon whether man chose to disobey God (Genesis 2:17). The sad fact is that our first parents did choose to sin, and part of the punishment was the subjection of the entire race to physical death. See Genesis 3:19; Romans 5:12; 8:10. Thus death is not a natural part of our existence. It is an enemy (1 Corinthians 15:26) and a proper object of fear for sinners (Hebrews 2:14, 15).

The worst thing about death is not the event as such, but rather the fact that it is part of the total curse upon sin, which culminates in the eternal punishment of the second death (Revelation 20:14, 15; 21:8). The reason men fear to die is that they know it is the threshold to the judgment hall of God: "It is appointed for men to die once, and after this comes judgment" (Hebrews 9:27). That is fearsome unless we are forgiven.

One of the greatest dangers in the debate over euthanasia is that this Bible truth will be lost. Especially in a situation where a person is suffering unbearable pain, it is easy to begin to think of death as a friend, as a blessing to be welcomed. For instance, a pamphlet issued by the Euthanasia Educational Council is entitled "Do Doctors Know the Real Enemy?" It tells the story of an old man with many ailments who suffered a severe heart attack, only to be revived and kept alive by a lot of intensive-care machines. He wanted to die; he had requested to be allowed to die—but the doctors were trying to save him. In the night he turned off his own ventilator and expired, but he left this note: "Death is not the enemy, doctor. Inhumanity is."

This is typical of the way the euthanasia debate is making us insensitive to the evils of death. It just is not true to say that death is not an enemy. No matter how severe the bodily suffering, and no matter how degrading the indignity and "inhumanity" borne in one's last days, these are as nothing compared to the eternal suffering awaiting the sinner beyond death's door. Thus the word *euthanasia* is a misnomer: death is *not good*.

The second Biblical truth is somewhat of a qualification of the first one: *the enemy death has been defeated by Jesus Christ*. Part of the work of our Lord was to deliver us from the curse and fear of death, through His own death and resurrection. See Hebrews 2:14, 15; 2 Timothy 1:10. He faced our common enemy, death, and dealt it a mortal blow. See Revelation 1:18.

Thus, even though death is an enemy, for Christ *and* for those who receive His salvation it is a *defeated* enemy. The Christian still must die, but he does not fear death because he knows its "sting" of eternal punishment is gone (1 Corinthians 15:55-57), and because he knows he will be given a new body on the day of resurrection.

This means that a Christian looks at death and anticipates death in a way entirely different from the way of the unbeliever. Though death per se is not good, still for the Christian it may be preferable and even desirable in comparison with a large number of circumstances in this life. In fact, the Christian's death is *always* good in that it brings his living soul into the very presence of the Redeemer. Thus Paul could say that "to die is gain," and that it is "very much better" to depart and be with Christ (Philippians 1:21-23). See 2 Corinthians 5:1-8.

When Paul said these things, he was not enduring any kind of intense persecution or suffering, as far as we know. Thus if death is "very much better" for the Christian even in good times, certainly it can be welcomed in times of great pain and irrecoverable deterioration. We *must* remember, though, that the *only* reason a Christian can face death without terror is that he shares in Christ's victory over this enemy. This is not true of sinners. This means that the options for Christians may be different from those of unbelievers at times.

A third Biblical truth about death is that *murder is sinful*. God has forbidden us deliberately to take another person's life (or our own): "You shall not murder" (Exodus 20:13). We cannot presume to suspend the sixth Commandment for any reason. It is not our prerogative to make exceptions; God alone is the Lord of life and death. Murder is murder, even when the end being sought is the relief of the victim. The "right to die" does not include the right to murder (or to commit suicide), even when death is better.

The last Biblical truth about death is directly related to the preceding one: we have the right to cause the death of another human being *only* when that person has been judged "worthy of death" by a governmental decision (Acts 25:11; Romans 13:4). This involves only those who are guilty of evildoing; *all innocent life is protected by the sixth Commandment*.

This is especially important since in the euthanasia debate one often hears such terms as "the quality of life" and "meaningful life." The idea is that the life remaining for some people is judged to be meaningless or of such low quality that it is not worth living. In such situations euthanasia is advocated by many.

One very practical problem with this is the presumption involved in judging for another whether his life is worth living. Related to this is the question of who along the way will be making the decisions as to whose life is worth living or not. The potential for tyranny here is frightening.

But even apart from these practical considerations is the truth that guilt or innocence is the only determining factor in the taking of human life. As one writer has said, "The biblical standard is not 'meaningfulness' but *innocence*."

II. Active and Passive Euthanasia

In light of the Biblical truths explained above it is possible to draw some definite conclusions regarding euthanasia. The first is that what is commonly called "active euthanasia" is an act of murder and is *never* right.

Active euthanasia is the term applied to a situation in which someone takes deliberate action (an act of commission) to end the life of a person in distress. An example of this, as reported by a national news magazine, is the case of George Z., 26, who became paralyzed from the neck down because of a motorcycle accident. He felt his life was useless, and he begged his brother Lester, 23, to kill him. Lester complied, with a shotgun at short range.

Another example is the case of Dr. G., who was put on trial for administering a lethal dose of morphine to her seventy-eight-year-old mother, who was dying a slow and painful death. The mother requested her daughter to put her out of her misery, and Dr. G. granted the request. We can sympathize even if we cannot approve.

Sometimes active euthanasia is self-administered, in which case it is simply suicide. In 1975 a well-known liberal theologian and his wife, Dr. and Mrs. Henry Van Dusen, ages seventy-seven and eighty, decided they no longer wanted to endure their uncomfortable physical conditions. They were not in unbearable pain, but were both "increasingly weak and unwell," as their suicide note put it. They took overdoses of sleeping pills together.

In spite of our deep sympathy toward these individuals and others in similar circumstances, we cannot avoid the conclusion that it is never right deliberately to kill an innocent person. Judgements as to whether a particular life is meaningless, useless, or worthless are irrelevant. Also they are often wrong, as in the case of George Z. True, he faced a tragically dependent life; but such a life surrendered to God can be worthwhile and useful in many ways, as the example of Joni Eareckson shows. (See her books, *Joni* and *A Step Further,* Zondervan, 1976 and 1978.)

The other conclusion has to do with *passive euthanasia,* which is the term applied to most situations in which someone intentionally takes an innocent life by deliberately *withholding* whatever is necessary to keep the person alive. It is called "passive" because no active steps are taken to kill the person; it is rather an act of omission. It is called "euthanasia," though, because the purpose of the withholding is to hasten the sufferer's death.

At this point two important distinctions are usually made. One is the distinction between *ordinary* and *extraordinary* medical procedures. The former are the more or less routine operations and treatments; the latter are excessively painful or expensive treatments whose benefit is questionable anyway. The other distinction is that between a deteriorating situation from which there is *hope of recovery,* and a situation from which there is *no* hope of recovery. (Needless to say, it is not always easy to decide which is which.)

With these distinctions in mind we can set forth another definite conclusion: it is *never* right to withhold ordinary treatment and basic necessities (i.e., food, water, and air) from an innocent person, even when there is no hope of recovery. (If there *is* hope of recovery, it is never right to withhold even extraordinary treatment.)

Examples of such passive euthanasia include most cases of infanticide, which is a more common practice than most of us realize. Very often, when a baby is born with some type of serious birth defect such as Down's Syndrome (mongolism), the doctors and nurses, with parental consent, place the baby in a dark corner of the hospital nursery and allow it to die. They do not actually kill it, but they do nothing to keep it alive: they do not feed it or give it water, and they do not give it ordinary medical treatment.

A few years ago a Florida legislator introduced a bill into the state legislature which would have permitted state institutions to withhold ordinary treatment from retarded persons suffering from treatable illnesses such as pneumonia. The purpose was to bring about as many deaths as possible so as to save the cost of keeping such persons in the institutions.

These situations are heart-rending *and* expensive, to be sure, but we must conclude that *causing* death in such cases is wrong, whether it be by something done or not done. There is no moral difference between active and passive euthanasia. Both are violations of the sixth Commandment; both are murder.

III. What About "No-Hope" Situations?

Certain dilemmas arise when we encounter those who are suffering from irreversible deterioration or are in situations from which there is no hope of recovery. This may involve a patient who has incurred brain damage and is in a coma without expectation of regaining consciousness. It may be a newborn infant with a grotesque birth defect. Or it may be a person in full command of his senses, suffering from cancer or heart disease, who knows he will not survive long anyway, and for whom all continued attempts to keep him alive are themselves agonizing or only serve to prolong his agony.

The general rule in such situations is this: where hope for recovery is gone, no *extraordinary* means need to be used to *prolong death*. This does not apply, of course, to vital necessities. Even for patients in irreversible comas, we cannot withhold air, nourishment, and water. Nor does it apply to ordinary treatments, such as antibiotics and painkillers. But we are not morally required to continue extremely painful or expensive treatments where the only result is prolonging the moment of death, often while the patient continues to suffer. Such withholding of extraordinary means in no-hope situations is *not* euthanasia and is not morally wrong.

A few years ago I spoke on this subject at a church in Indiana. Afterwards an elderly Christian lady, Mrs. C., told me that she was suffering from a disease which was gradually becoming worse and which would ultimately kill her. There was no cure, but a specific kind of operation could prolong her life for a little longer. She had already undergone this operation several times and had found it to be an increasingly terrible ordeal. Her question was this: would it be wrong for her to decide *not* to have the operation again, even though she would probably die sooner? My answer, in accord with the principle stated in the previous paragraph, was that it would not be wrong.

I have a friend whose wife, Mrs. R., suffered serious brain damage as the result of an accident. The doctor had just informed him that she would never recover consciousness, but that her body could be kept functioning by being attached to a life support system—if he so chose. He asked me if I thought it would be wrong *not* to request that this be done. Since Mrs. R. was a Christian lady, my answer was that if there truly was no hope for recovery (this is *not* an easy determination to make), then there is no moral obligation to keep the body functioning through such extraordinary means.

In view of the Biblical truths discussed in the first section of this chapter, one exception must be made to the approach to "no-hope" cases presented here. If we are confronted with a situation like that of Mrs. R., where the patient is comatose with no hope of attaining consciousness, then no extraordinary means need be employed whether the person is a believer or an unbeliever. *But,* if we are dealing with a case like that of Mrs. C., where the patient is still conscious or can be restored to consciousness, then even extraordinary means should be used to keep the person alive—*if he is not a Christian.*

The Christian can forgo heroic measures in these cases because for him, "to die is gain." But to the unforgiven sinner, death and the judgment that follows are a terror far greater than bodily pain and indignity. Thus in cases where the decision depends on us, we should do all we can to prolong life if that will give the sinner further opportunity to accept Christ as Savior. In every situation "death with hope" is a greater value to be sought than "death with dignity."

In the days to come we can expect to witness more intensive efforts to have euthanasia gain acceptability and be legalized, especially in its passive form. It may well be up to Christians to take the lead in holding the line with regard to respect for human life.

10

Human Engineering

One thing that most people agree on is that mankind today is not what it should be, and that certain changes or "improvements" could be made. We would probably not agree, though, on the *kinds* of changes that should be made. Herein lies one of the more unusual ethical problems of our time.

No longer than a generation ago this subject would not have been discussed in a book like this, because on a practical level the problem simply did not exist. The kinds of changes that could be made in human nature were rather limited. Rapid advances in the world of science, however, have altered the situation.

For instance, here are some "little known facts about the biological revolution," as listed in a recent book advertisement: Dr. E. A. Carlson of UCLA believes that there may be enough DNA remaining in the King Tut mummy for scientists to clone an exact living copy of the ancient ruler. One company has actually experimented with changing the human digestive tract so that people could eat and digest hay, like cows. There are now at least eight different laboratory methods to make a baby besides the normal one. Top genetic engineers discuss doubling the human brain size in order to produce a new super species of man. Dr. Kimball Atwood of the University of Illinois says there is no reason why animals and plants could not be genetically crossed so that skin, like leaves, could perform photosynthesis.

This is what is known as "human engineering." These are the kinds of changes that are being made possible by modern science. *The fact that something is possible, however, does not mean that it is right.* We must ask what kinds of changes in human nature are right or morally permissible in the light of Scripture.

I. Possible Procedures

So that the full scope of the problem may be known, we will now present a systematic survey with brief explanations of the kinds of procedures being attempted in the quest to modify man.

A. Genetic Research

The first category has to do with genes, those minute units of chromosomes that control heredity. In recent years they have been the object of intense research, and our understanding of how they function is constantly increasing. At this time several procedures are possible.

First of all, it is now possible to *identify* a large number of defective genes. (This is important since about 2,500 maladies can now be traced to genetic defects.) For instance, it is often possible to determine whether a prospective parent has a genetic problem that is likely to be transmitted to any offspring. If such is the case, this person may then opt to be sterilized, with children being obtained by adoption.

Other possible options include several one-parent methods of child-bearing, such as artificial insemination of a genetically-normal wife from an anonymous donor (called A.I.D.). Also, many believe that it will soon be possible to produce a child from either parent by cloning.

Genetic defects can also be detected in unborn babies while they are still growing in the womb. This is done through a process called amniocentesis, or an analysis of the baby's sloughed-off cells suspended in the amniotic fluid. If such an examination shows that the baby has a genetic deformity (such as Down's Syndrome), the parents are given the choice of having an abortion.

A second procedure made possible by genetic research is the actual *repairing* of defective genes. This is the result of the development of a number of techniques whereby sound genetic material from a normal cell can be transplanted into cells with faulty genes.

Duane Gish and Clifford Wilson describe how this might be done for a patient with sickle cell anemia (in *Manipulating Life;* San Diego: Master Books, 1981; pp. 124-5). Tissue that produces red blood cells would be removed from the patient and grown in a cell culture. "The genes that code for hemoglobin production would be obtained from a normal healthy individual and inserted into the defective cells of the patient," who then might produce enough normal hemoglobin to survive.

A third possible procedure in the area of genetic research is the *combining* of genetic material (DNA) from different life-forms in order to produce unusual hybrids. Potentially almost any combination is possible, though the result would ordinarily be just a mass of cells in a laboratory dish rather than some monster that was half carrot and half tiger.

Some hybrids have actually been produced; however, these are usually new variations of a particular type of bacteria. For instance, by combining the proper human genetic material with the genes of E. coli bacteria, new strains of E. coli can be produced which will "manufacture," by simple cell multiplication, natural human chemicals such as insulin and interferon. The latter is used to fight certain types of cancer, but is usually very difficult to obtain. (See Lane Lester, *Cloning;* Wheaton: Tyndale House, 1980; p. 128.)

B. The Reproductive Process

Another avenue for modifying man involves variations in the reproductive process. For instance, numerous kinds of selective mating have long been discussed, and some have been attempted on a limited scale. This is called *eugenics,* and the goal is to improve the overall quality of the human race. This may be done in a negative way, by preventing any "undesirable" types from reproducing, e.g., by forced sterilization. Some leading scientists have proposed that only people with "superior" genotypes be licensed to have babies.

A positive approach to eugenics would encourage "superior" types to mate with one another without necessarily prohibiting others from reproducing. Hitler attempted such a program in order to produce his concept of a master race. A man in California is attempting, via artificial insemination, to pair Nobel Prize-winners with women of supreme intelligence for the same purpose. Some have suggested the establishment of frozen sperm and/or egg banks, from which prospective parents could select according to their choice of characteristics.

Other variations in the reproductive process are designed to overcome barriers to child-bearing in certain cases. For instance, a technique already developed is "test-tube" fertilization. If a woman is unable to ovulate normally, a number of her egg cells are surgically removed and fertilized in a laboratory dish with her husband's sperm. A fertilized ovum is then inserted into the womb for normal development. Several babies have been born by this method.

Another artificial method of reproduction is cloning. In this procedure offspring may be produced from a single parent, male or female, by manipulating the nucleus of a body cell from the parent. Barring complications the offspring will be the genetic duplicate of the parent. (This has been done with some plants and animals; no cases of human cloning have been documented yet.)

C. Behavior Control

A third avenue for modifying individuals is behavior control. This can be done by several means. One means is psychological techniques such as brainwashing and behavior modification. Another is the chemical or electrical stimulation of the brain. A third is some type of surgical procedure on the brain (i.e., psychosurgery).

Modern brain research has pinpointed the specific areas of the brain that control a large number of bodily functions as well as moods and emotions. By stimulating a particular spot with an implanted electrode, a specific action can be artificially produced. Or by destroying a small portion of a brain via surgery, certain kinds of undesirable behavior can be eliminated.

II. Ethical Problems

What should be the Christian's attitude toward these and other such possibilities in the area of the life sciences? Should we be concerned about them at all?

Of course we must be concerned. Relatively few of us will become directly involved in such projects, but sooner or later the decisions made on these issues will affect us all as they become matters of public policy. Thus it is imperative that Christians speak out now in order to influence these decisions from the perspective of God's Word.

A. Is the *Goal* Ethical?

As is the case with many ethical problems, the various forms of human engineering must be evaluated in terms of the END being sought and the MEANS used to achieve that end. First we must ask concerning the *end:* what are the researchers trying to achieve in their efforts to modify man? There are two main possibilities. Either they are trying to *correct defects* present in the world as the result of sin, or they are trying to *improve the species* of man.

In my judgment the former goal is consistent with the Bible and is ethically proper. When sin first entered, it turned the world upside down in more ways than one. Nature itself came into the grip of alien forces (Romans 8:20-22). This is especially true of man's physical nature, which was subjected to death because of sin (Romans 5:12-14; 8:10). Disease and defects are in a sense lesser forms of death. Other evils in the world also have been brought about by man's sin.

The question is this: are we permitted to try to fight and overcome these effects of sin? Or must we accept them without question as "God's will"? It is true that death is a God-appointed penalty for sin (Hebrews 9:27). But it is also true that God has provided redemption from this and other penalties, and He has permitted us to begin to taste of this redemption even in this life.

This is true even in the area of physical death. Normally we cannot hope to escape it completely, but we *can* fight it and forestall it. The many Biblical miracles of healing demonstrate this. Prayer for God's providential healing is proper (James 5:14, 15). The work of physicians such as Luke is not condemned (Colossians 4:14), nor is the use of medicines (Luke 10:34; 1 Timothy 5:23).

Thus any efforts to correct defects of this kind seem to be consistent with God's will. In principle we have already granted this in our support and use of doctors, medicine, hospitals, and research. There truly is nothing wrong with the goal of eliminating birth defects and genetic diseases, removing roadblocks to childbearing, or even altering behavior to eliminate undesirable activity. (We must not expect perfection until the second coming, though. See Romans 8:19-23.)

On the other hand, the goal of trying to improve the species is wrong because it usurps the role of the Creator and denies the nature of man as a creature designed by God. This applies to all efforts to redesign the race or create the "ideal" human being. For instance, genetic manipulation to create extra thumbs, extra stomachs, abnormally large brains, or legless bodies (for career astronauts) would be wrong.

This is truly "playing God," since it assumes that man has not been purposefully designed and made by an actual God but has rather come into existence by chance evolution. It also assumes that man himself, having attained self-consciousness and intelligence, is now capable of controlling his future evolution. After all, if everything, including man, is by nature in a state of flux and chance development, then why should we not engineer the changes ourselves? Why shouldn't we try to create the "man of the future" according to our own standards?

The reason, or course, is clear: *God is our Creator.* He made us, and pronounced the result "very good" (Genesis 1:26-31). We did not make ourselves (Psalms 100:3; 139:13-16). Trying to improve or redesign the race is a direct challenge to God's work and wisdom as Creator. We are warned not to attempt to usurp God's role in any way: Genesis 3:5; Isaiah 14:12-15; 45:9, 10; Ezekiel 28:1-10. Thus we must condemn this particular goal of human engineering.

B. Are the *Means* Ethical?

It is not always enough to evaluate the ethics of a particular end being sought; one must consider the *means* used to achieve it. Of course, if the end itself is wrong, then all means toward that end are wrong also. But what about a goal that is in itself good and proper? Here we must recognize that quite often, even though the end sought is acceptable, the means used to accomplish it is wrong. *Good ends do not justify bad means.*

For instance, even though the goal of having children is not wrong in itself (nor is it *necessary,* we might add), nevertheless most of the means being used to accomplish it outside the normal way are wrong. Test-tube fertilization as a means of child-bearing must be condemned because a single successful conception and birth are always accompanied by many experiments that do not succeed. A large number of ova are actually fertilized and begin to grow as new human beings, but most are either discarded or are not successfully transplanted into the womb. Thus usually scores of babies are killed in the effort to produce one.

Cloning presents similar problems. Even in experiments done thus far on animals, many deformed and aborted specimens have resulted from the efforts to produce a few good ones. (See Gish and Wilson, page 67.) The very nature of the process makes cell damage likely, and the minute size of human ova magnifies the problem. As Lester says, "Human cloning will not be attained without much trial and error and the destruction of numerous egg cells and human embryos. Some of the embryos may develop into clone 'monsters' before they die or are killed in the laboratory" (page 32).

No one who opposes abortion can consistently condone either of these means of reproduction.

Another example of wrong means toward right ends is any type of psychosurgery that modifies personality to such an extent that the patient no longer acts by choice and thus has no moral responsibility.

What about recombinant DNA techniques where human genetic material is added to bacteria to produce disease-fighting chemicals? In my judgement it is acceptable because the product of this genetic manipulation is not a new kind of man, and the end being sought is the proper one. (It is no different in principle from incorporating animal parts into the body to help correct certain defects, such as heart valves from pigs.)

Many questions about particular procedures must remain unanswered in this brief chapter, but we have attempted to explain and illustrate the method by which we should evaluate all such techniques in the light of the Bible, whether they be current or not yet discovered.

In all these efforts we must keep two things in mind. One, there is no substitute for the *new birth* as the God-appointed means for bringing about the most-needed changes in man in this age. Two, the New Humanity will not be finally achieved until the *new earth* has been established and we inhabit it in our resurrected bodies.

Racism

In the last few chapters we have been concerned with the integrity of human life. We have seen that the sixth Commandment, "You shall not murder," rules out the taking of innocent human life.

We have been dealing mostly with the physical aspect of man's life, but now it is time to remember that man is *spirit* also.

We are no more permitted to harm a man's spirit than we are his body. The Bible shows that to attack another person verbally or even mentally is a form of murder. Jesus says that murder includes hurling derogatory names and insults at someone (Matthew 5:21, 22). John reminds us that just hating another person makes us guilty of murder (1 John 3:15).

It is in this light that we must attempt to understand the sin of racism. It is a form of murder, an attack on the personhood and the humanness of a whole race, including every individual within that race. Thus it can be neither practiced nor condoned by anyone who wants to be within the will of God.

The defenders of racism often turn to the Bible itself in order to justify its practice. Thus it is necessary to clarify the Bible's teaching on this subject. That is our goal in this chapter.

I. Racial Superiority

The term *race* is defined in many ways. In its broadest sense it refers to any group of people who share a certain common characteristic, such as skin color, language, culture, or ancestry. More technically a race is a specific biological group that may be distinguished from other such groups by genetically transmitted differences. For our purposes it does not matter whether one is thinking in terms of the three or four or nine major races or in terms of the perhaps hundreds of smaller groups. Racism is racism, no matter how the racial group is defined.

What is racism? It is the judgment that one particular race or group of races is inherently *superior* to all others, or conversely that one particular race or group of races is inherently *inferior* to all others. This judgment is then used to justify attitudes and actions of intolerance and discrimination toward those of the "inferior" race.

Examples of racism abound. These include Hitler's exaltation of the so-called "Aryan" race and his attempt to exterminate the Jewish race. Alongside such hatred of the Jewish race (anti-Semitism) one could place all concepts of Jewish superiority. Another example is the notion of white superiority as over against blacks, Indians, or Chinese; still another is the Black Muslims' teaching of black superiority.

The real causes of such racist views are widely debated and in many cases unknown. Sometimes contrived reasons will be offered to justify existing pride or prejudice. These have included a race's alleged animal origin, innate tendency to immorality, or deficient mental ability. The ones that concern us most, however, are those that are supposedly based on the Bible.

Biblical support has been sought for both Jewish superiority and Jewish inferiority. Those who argue for the former point to Israel's role as God's chosen people and assume that this gives the Jews special status even today. They overlook two basic Bible teachings. First, God's original choice of the Jews had nothing to do with racial superiority, either as cause or as result. See Deuteronomy 7:6-8.

The only reason God singled out any nation at all for special service and honor was the need to prepare for the first coming of Christ into the world. Being chosen for this role gave Israel great privileges (Romans 3:1, 2; 9:4, 5), but this special status ceased once the work of preparation was completed. The Bible specifically states that the distinction between the Jews and the rest of mankind is no longer relevant. See Galatians 3:28, 29; Ephesians 2:14-16.

At the same time the Bible gives no ground for anti-Semitism, or discriminating *against* the Jews. They are no longer a special people; nevertheless the only reason why God has rejected any of them is their refusal to accept Jesus as the Christ. See Romans 10:1-3; 11:20. The Jews before Pilate's court did say, "His blood be on us and on our children" (Matthew 27:25); but there is no evidence that God himself has put a perpetual curse on the Jews for their participation in the crucifixion of Christ. Jews who reject Jesus today are no worse than non-Jews who reject Him, and Jewish Christians are one with non-Jewish Christians.

Another common misuse of the Bible in defense of racism is the appeal to the so-called Hamitic curse in Genesis 9:22-25. Without any justification whatsoever this passage has been asserted to teach (1) that Ham's descendants are the black race, (2) that the black race is cursed, (3) that their blackness is a result of the curse, (4) that the cursed black race is condemned to be slaves, and (5) that all of this is ordained by God.

All this is racist mythology; it is definitely not taught in Genesis 9. (See Thomas Figart, *A Biblical Perspective on the Race Problem;* Baker, 1973; pp. 53-62.)

Most alleged biological grounds for racism have no basis in fact, either, such as the fantasy that some races were created by God while others descended from animals and thus are not really human. Of course there are some biological or genetic differences among the races. But such differences, even if they extend to such factors as higher or lower intellectual capacity, do not affect the dignity of any race, since *all* races are God's creatures and are created in His own image. None is superior; none in inferior.

II. Racial Segregation

One expression of racism is the insistence on racial segregation. Sometimes even where racial superiority or inferiority is not actually asserted, a segregation of the races is advocated. Such segregation may take many forms, from the extreme of total separation (even on separate continents) to the prohibition of intermarriage.

Again many proponents of racial segregation argue that their view is taught in the Bible and that segregation thus is shown to be God's will. In this section we will present a brief survey of Bible passages used to support this view. We shall see, contrary to the thinking of some very sincere people, that these passages cannot legitimately be used to support segregation.

The first such passage is the so-called "table of nations" in Genesis 10. This passage lists some of the descendants of Shem, Ham, and Japheth; and it tells which parts of the post-flood world were settled by them. Genesis 10:32 concludes, "These are the families of the sons of Noah, according to their genealogies, by their nations; and out of these the nations were separated on the earth after the flood." The occasion for the dispersion is recorded in Genesis 11.

This passage is usually cited in connection with Acts 17:26, which says, "And He made from one every nation of mankind to live on all the face of the earth, having determined their appointed times, and the boundaries of their habitation."

From these passages some have drawn the conclusion that God deliberately dispersed the earth's population along racial lines; therefore any attempt at integration of races is against God's will.

Several things must be said about this conclusion. First, neither Genesis 10 and 11 nor Acts 17:26 says anything at all about a separation of *races*. The divisions are made according to family groups, languages, and nations. Just how the races fit into these groupings is not clear, and it is likely that some groups are not named at all. If the actions taken in these passages require segregation, it must be according to political boundaries and languages. The fact is that they are not patterns or mandates for segregation at all.

Second, the problem that caused the dispersion of the earth's population in Genesis 11 was not racial but spiritual. The dispersion was not intended to segregate races but to prevent spiritual degradation. It was done according to language, not race.

Third, Acts 17:26 is speaking of God's providential control over the continuing fortunes of nations as political units. The rise and fall of kings and nations are in His hands. The Babylons and the Romes arise at their "appointed times" to serve His spiritual purposes; their boundaries expand or shrink according to His plan. There is no specific reference to race here; there is certainly no exclusive reference to Genesis 10 and 11.

Other passages sometimes used to support racial segregation are those in which God warns the Israelites not to mix with the pagan population in and around the land of Canaan. These include Exodus 34:11-16 and Deuteronomy 7:1-4. For instance, Exodus 34:12 says, "Watch yourself that you make no covenant with the inhabitants of the land." Also, says Deuteronomy 7:3, 4, "You shall not intermarry with them; you shall not give your daughters to their sons, nor shall you take their daughters for your sons. For they will turn your sons away from following Me to serve other gods."

It is true that God did command the Israelites to segregate themselves from their neighbors. But the point was *spiritual* purity, not racial purity. Mixing and even intermarriage were allowed if the alien was a proselyte or if no spiritual threat ensued. Moses himself married a "Cushite woman" (Numbers 12:1), a descendant of Ham (Genesis 10:6); and one of Jesus' own ancestors was Rahab, presumably a Canaanite, and thus another descendant of Ham!

The New Testament parallel to the spiritual segregation imposed upon Israel is God's command to Christians today not to "be bound together with unbelievers," for "what has a believer in common with an unbeliever? . . . 'Therefore, come out from their midst and be separate,' says the Lord" (2 Corinthians 6:14-17).

Our conclusion must be that there is no Biblical teaching that refers strictly to racial segregation. It is one of those issues on which the Bible is silent. A major principle of Biblical interpretation is that *we* must be silent where the Bible is silent; i.e., we must not manufacture commandments where the Bible gives none.

It must also be noted that in those matters where the Bible is silent, the rule of expediency applies: "All things are lawful for me, but not all things are profitable" (1 Corinthians 6:12). There may be times and places where some form of segregation is the best expression of neighbor-love, or where it is the least hindrance to witness and service for Christ.

This applies especially to interracial marriage. We cannot say that God's Word prohibits marriage between persons of different races. However, as with all subjects about which the Bible is silent, we must ask in each individual case, "Is it expedient?" In some cultures and some areas of the world, no social stigma is attached to interracial marriage; so no ill results are likely to follow. But in places and cultures where such marriages are socially taboo, a Christian must consider questions such as the following: How will this act affect my witness for Christ? Will it be a stumbling block for weaker brethren? Will the children resulting from this union be subjected to social persecution? Is this in the best interests of love *(agape,* not *eros)?* We are obligated to answer such questions honestly and to submit ourselves to the most expedient course of action.

III. Racial Solidarity

Over against man's tendencies to fragment humankind into opposing groups lies the Bible's emphasis on the solidarity of the race. This is the perspective that must shape our own attitude toward other races.

All human beings of all races have a single biological origin. God created one original pair, Adam and Eve, from which all of humanity has sprung. "He made from one every nation of mankind to live on all the face of the earth" (Acts 17:26). Some manuscripts say "from one blood."

All human beings thus share the same nature, both biological and spiritual. All are made in God's image (Genesis 1:26, 27). This means that all have the same inherent dignity and worth. All likewise have corrupted the divine image through sin; thus all share the same shame and degradation. Herein are ruled out all concepts of superiority and inferiority.

Solidarity is further seen in the fact that all human beings are equally the objects of God's love (Matthew 5:44, 45; John 3:16). This is seen in the fact that Jesus died for all persons of all races: He is the propitiation for the sins of "the whole world" (1 John 2:2).

The fact of the matter is that God does not make distinctions among races or even individuals: "God is not one to show partiality, but in every nation the man who fears Him and does what is right, is welcome to Him" (Acts 10:34, 35).

Nowhere should this racial solidarity be more obvious than in the church. Above all others the people of God should acknowledge and model the fact that "there is no distinction between Greek and Jew, circumcised and uncircumcised, barbarian, Scythian, slave and freeman" (Colossians 3:11). Since this is the way it is for God, how can we look at it any differently? If God loves all races and cares for all races alike, how can we do less? The fires of racial hatred must be replaced by a genuine, all-encompassing love like God's very own.

12

Anger

"Did you ever lose your temper?"

"I guess not, since I still seem to have it all."

We chuckle at this, and wince at the same time, because anger is an ethical problem with which we are all too familiar.

Anger is a spiritual attitude, a state of mind. Specifically it is a strong feeling of displeasure against a real or supposed wrong, accompanied by an urge to retaliate in some way against the wrong. Thus it seldom occurs as an isolated event, but usually leads to action of some kind.

Anger is condemned as a sin: "Let all bitterness and wrath and anger . . . be put away from you," says Ephesians 4:31. In Matthew 5:21, 22 Jesus compares anger toward a brother with murder itself.

At the same time, the Bible does not forbid *all* expressions of anger. In fact, it teaches that a properly motivated and directed anger is a necessary part of Christian character. In the very same context where Paul warns against "wrath and anger," he gives this admonition: "Be angry, and yet do not sin; do not let the sun go down on your anger, and do not give the devil an opportunity" (Ephesians 4:26, 27).

How can we "be angry," and yet not sin? We find the answer to this question in the nature of *God's* anger. In this part of Ephesians 4 Paul is describing what it means to be created in God's image, or more specifically what it means for a sinner to be *renewed* in God's image. Our character must be like God's character. Our anger must be patterned after God's anger.

As we examine this subject further, two propositions will emerge: first, holy anger is essential for a godly character; second, this holy anger must be tempered with holy love.

I. Holy Anger: a Necessity

"Be angry, and yet do not sin." Some think that Paul is adapting the words of Psalm 4:4 to express this principle. Whether the first part of this statement be taken as a direct command or not, the principle is clear: Christian character does include an anger that is not sinful.

What is the difference between holy anger and unholy anger? In some ways the Christian's anger is not different from that which is forbidden in Ephesians 4:31. It is the same basic passion. The difference between them, so that one is permissible—even essential—while the other is forbidden, has to do with their origin and object.

The two kinds of anger are aroused by different motives and are controlled by different spirits. The Christian is a new man. He is no longer motivated by greed, lust, vanity, pride, or selfishness. He is made in the likeness of God. The very ground from which his anger springs is different from that of the sinner.

The sinner's heart and life are self-centered. Therefore his anger springs from selfish motives such as personal jealousy or wounded pride. It is directed against other persons in a spirit of retaliation, and it seeks revenge for personal wrongs.

For example, when Cain's offering was pronounced inferior to Abel's, his wounded pride and his selfish jealousy resulted in murderous anger. (See Genesis 4:3-8.) When David received more praise than Saul, Saul's jealousy begat within him the angry hatred that ruined his own life. (See 1 Samuel 18:7-9.) When Mordecai refused to bow to the haughty Haman, it was Haman's wrath that wove for Mordecai the noose that fell on Haman's own neck. (See Esther 3:5.)

The Christian's heart is different, and so is his life. No longer is it self-centered. It is God-centered. We look at things through God's eyes and with God's heart, seeing what God sees and feeling what God feels. Our wrath is stirred at what stirs God's wrath.

This leads to the question of the proper object of wrath. What kinds of things make God angry? When we see this, then we shall know the nature of that holy wrath that is essential to Christian character.

Very simply, God's wrath is always directed against sin, or against that which is contrary to His nature and law. It is the expression of His holy jealousy for sole and complete obedience. At Canaan's border Moses admonished Israel: "You shall not follow other gods, any of the gods of the peoples who surround you, for the Lord your God in the midst of you is a jealous God; otherwise the anger of the Lord your God will be kindled against you, and He will wipe you off the face of the earth" (Deuteronomy 6:14, 15). Idolatry is wrong, and therefore it makes God angry.

We see an illustration of this divine wrath as it was directed against Israel at Sinai. In the very midst of covenant-making, Israel had set up a golden calf against God's express command (Exodus 20:4). God's response is recorded in Exodus 32:9, 10: "I have seen this people, and behold, they are an obstinate people. Now then let Me alone, that My anger may burn against them, and that I may destroy them."

The nature of holy anger is revealed in the person of Christ. In Mark 3:5 we read of Jesus' anger against the hypocritical, hardhearted Pharisees. In Matthew 21:12 we see His anger expressed against the mercenary, materialistic temple keepers.

What conclusions may we draw regarding the holy anger of Christians? First, we see that holy anger is directed against sin and springs from a jealousy for the sovereignty of God, not personal jealousy. We cannot be angry for ourselves; we must be angry for God's sake.

A caution must be urged, however. We must be careful not to mistake personal offenses and wounded pride for the offended honor of God. Let us not pour out our passion on petty things or personal things. Someone leaves a beer bottle in the street; we run over it and get a flat tire. We then become so angry—at the stupid so-and-so who caused us to have to change a tire in the rain. Perhaps more appropriate objects of our wrath would be the sins of drunkenness and lawlessness as forms of rebellion against the authority of God. We cannot let personal inconveniences sap the passion that should be expended upon sins against God.

Second, we conclude that such holy anger against sin is necessary for Christian character and especially for the Christian minister. We cannot have a cold heart toward sin! We cannot be calloused and unmoved at the things that stir the heart of God! The man who is unmoved by the sight of sin and disobedience and injustice is little better than the man who indulges in them.

The very thought of the power of sin and death in the world ought to rouse within us fire and zeal and passion against it. When Jesus approached the tomb of Lazarus, He wept not only in sorrow and in sympathy with Mary and Martha, but also in burning rage against the violent tyranny of Satan, the author of death, whose powers were so evident at that time. (See John 11:33-38.) We, too, must be enraged in the spirit as we encounter the effects of the evil one. We must be stirred with a fury that leads to action!

This leads to another question. What sort of action should be the result of this holy anger? Should we be like James and John, who wanted to call down fire from heaven upon an unbelieving Samaritan village? Or should we rather be like Jesus, who rebuked His rash apostles and steadfastly set His face toward Jerusalem, bound for the cross upon which He would die for those unbelieving Samaritans? (See Luke 9:51-56.)

This leads to our second point, namely, that holy anger must be tempered with holy love.

II. Tempered With Holy Love

"Do not let the sun go down on your anger." We see here that we are to have our anger under complete control. We must never be subject to fits of rage; we must not "lose our temper." When we become angry, we must be able to turn the burner down, so to speak, and set our wrath aside on the same day in which it arises.

Some see in Paul's command a reference to Psalm 4:4, "Meditate in your heart upon your bed, and be still." There can be no real stillness of conscience, no good night's sleep while anger burns within us.

Others see a reference to Deuteronomy 24:13, 15, where the law requires that certain accounts be settled by sundown. In any case, the imagery is quite appropriate: the calming effect of night's quiet should be felt upon our tempers each day. As the day's heat cools down with the setting of the sun, so should the fires of our anger disappear over the horizon with it.

How is this possible? How can holy anger stop short of the execution of righteous judgment and vengeance upon the wicked? By its being tempered with love, mercy, and kindness. "Put on a heart of compassion, kindness, humility, gentleness and patience; bearing with one another, and forgiving each other, whoever has a complaint against any one. . . . And beyond all these things put on love, which is the perfect bond of unity" (Colossians 3:12-14).

Holy anger springs from the soil of a new heart created in God's likeness, and God is a God of love as well as a God of wrath. Indeed, His love surpasses His wrath. God truly is jealous with a fiery wrath for His sovereignty, but He is also loving and merciful even to idolatrous covenant-breakers. God revealed himself to Moses after the apostasy at Sinai. How did he describe himself? As a God wrathful and vengeful? No! "Then the Lord passed by in front of him and proclaimed, 'The Lord, the Lord God, compassionate and gracious, slow to anger, and abounding in lovingkindness and truth; who keeps lovingkindness for thousands, who forgives iniquity, transgression and sin; yet He will by no means leave the guilty unpunished" (Exodus 34:6, 7).

As Christ reveals the character of God, again we see holy anger tempered with holy love. Following a scathing sermon against the hypocritical Pharisees, probably the very ones with whom He had been angry earlier (Mark 3:5; Matthew 21:12), He concluded not with something like, "You all deserve to go to Hell and I hope you do!" He lamented instead, "O Jerusalem, Jerusalem, who kills the prophets and stones those who are sent to her! How often I wanted to gather your children together, the way a hen gathers her chicks under her wings, and you were unwilling" (Matthew 23:37).

Thus we may conclude that when holy anger springs from the heart of the Christian, who is made in the likeness of God, it must spring from a heart of love. Now we can see what kind of action should result from our holy anger: evangelism! Who are we, sinners saved by grace, to hold the hot torch of indignation against a lost sinner?

Holy anger against sin, tempered with a holy love for the sinner, should lead the minister to be more diligent in sermon preparation; it should lead each Christian to be more zealous in personal evangelism, to be more persistent in prayer, to be more active in public crusades against social evils. In all this we must be motivated by a heart of love and compassion that desires the salvation of the persons whose sin we hate.

"Do not let the sun go down on your anger." Simply holding the burning anger in our consciousness will not solve any problems. But when it immediately motivates us to a labor of love, then our passions are being rightly controlled.

"And do not give the devil an opportunity." When anger is harbored in the heart and is not transformed by love into zealous action, then the devil has gained a foothold for reentry into our lives. For anger leads so readily to harsh words, blows, grudges, alienation of friends, tears, hatred, strife, revenge, murder, lost souls. This shows the need for settling all disagreements with our brethren at once. This shows the need for channeling passion against sin into efforts of evangelism. It shows the need, the great need, for tempering holy anger with holy love.

Pride

A proud heart is sin, says the wise man (Proverbs 21:4); and "a man's pride will bring him low" (Proverbs 29:23). "God is opposed to the proud," says James 4:6. An oft-quoted (or misquoted) verse of Scripture says, "Pride goes before destruction, and a haughty spirit before stumbling" (Proverbs 16:18). As Dwight L. Moody paraphrases it, "Be humble, or you'll stumble."

There is a legitimate kind of pride, the kind that is manifested when a person "takes pride in" something to which he is related and for which he is responsible, such as his work, his church, his family, or his country. But there is also the kind of pride that is evil, indeed, that is considered by many to be chief of sins, the deadliest of the "seven deadly sins." C. S. Lewis has said, "Unchastity, anger, greed, drunkenness, and all that are mere flea bites in comparison with pride." This deadly sin is the more dangerous because the one who is guilty of it may not realize that he is proud.

What is pride? How can one know whether he has a proud heart? What attitudes reveal a proud heart? These are the things we need to know so that we may avoid this most deadly of sins. This chapter seeks to provide a guide for self-examination by suggesting several of the forms that pride may take. Then in closing it makes some suggestions for overcoming pride.

I. Self-importance

First, pride may manifest itself as a feeling of self-importance. Pride causes a person to have too high an opinion of himself; it causes him to think he is the *best:* the best looking, the best thinker, the best speaker, the best leader, the best worker, the best athlete. The sin may not necessarily lie in one's evaluation of himself as the best, for it may well be that he *is*. The sin of pride lies in attributing this superiority to one's own powers and in seeking personal credit for it and personal glory from it.

Such pride is certainly a prelude to destruction when it causes one to feel equal to and independent from God. Consider the case of Nebuchadnezzar, whose "heart was lifted up, and his spirit became so proud that he behaved arrogantly" (Daniel 5:20). As he reflected upon his reign in the royal city of Babylon, as recorded in Daniel 4:30, "the king reflected and said, 'Is this not Babylon the great, which I myself have built . . . by the might of my power and for the glory of my majesty?' " But while he was still speaking, the Lord announced to him that his kingdom was taken away from him, and that he should be a spectacle of madness until he humbled his spirit and learned the lesson that pride precedes destruction. See Daniel 4:31-37.

Other examples of destructive pride are Belshazzar (Daniel 5:22-30) and Herod (Acts 12:21-23).

These examples serve as a warning to all who are tempted by this feeling of self-importance and self-sufficiency to lift themselves up against God and to declare themselves to be independent of His reign. Such pride leads to literal destruction from the face of God, who shows us the folly of proclaiming, "I am the master of my fate; I am the captain of my soul."

But the feeling of self-importance leads to destruction in other areas, too. It leads inevitably to deterioration of relationships with other people. This is true because pride as self-importance causes one constantly to *compare* himself with others and to judge himself to be superior. Thus when one is convinced of his own self-importance, he will always consider his own opinions and suggestions and solutions to be the best and the wisest. For instance, in a committee or board meeting he will have difficulty seeing the merits of other people's suggestions, and may even look with scorn on them. As Proverbs 21:24 says, " 'Proud,' 'Haughty,' 'Scoffer,' are his names who acts with insolent pride." When others do not immediately extol his own views and opinions, he is resentful and suspicious; and if his opinion is rejected in favor of another, he becomes uncooperative and perhaps even disruptive. How many organizations, church boards, and even churches themselves have been rent apart just because someone did not get his own way? This is pride's destructive work.

The pride of self-importance leads to broken relationships in other ways. The desire to enhance one's own image causes him to rejoice in the mistakes and weaknesses of others. The more he can magnify their failures, the better he looks by comparison. The proud heart delights to humiliate or "to get the best of" someone else, or to "show him up." At the same time, the proud person becomes jealous and resentful if the other person excels, threatening to make the proud one only "number two." Thus he begins to look upon others as potential rivals and to do all he can to keep them down through malicious gossip or degrading remarks, for example.

It is very true, then, that pride leads to destruction. It destroys our relationships with others; it destroys good will. The proud heart will not be able to get along very well with others. Truly the wise man is right: "By pride cometh only contention" (Proverbs 13:10, American Standard Version).

II. Self-Justification

Pride also manifests itself as self-justification. This means it causes us to be defensive concerning our weaknesses and mistakes, our errors and sins. Pride compels us to justify ourselves in the sight of men even when we know we are wrong. It causes us to excuse ourselves and to deny errors.

Whenever we do make a bad mistake or commit a great sin, it is pride that causes us to try in every possible way to justify ourselves and to avoid the blame. We make all kinds of excuses. We try to shift the blame to someone else, or we call attention to someone else's weaknesses. We deny that we have done anything wrong. Our image must be protected at all costs!

Pride therefore makes it very difficult for us to accept criticism and correction, even when we know it is deserved. We become defensive when accused. We become angry when anyone calls attention to our errors and sins. We should be grateful and repentant, but we become indignant instead. Any admission of error, any admission that change is necessary, implies a prior weakness or poor judgment; it reflects badly upon our competence and ability. Thus pride can cause us to perpetuate a mistake.

Particularly susceptible to such pride are those in positions of responsibility or authority. A teacher may find it impossible to grant the validity of a student's criticisms and may turn upon him and attempt to humiliate him in return. A president or a director or a manager may perpetuate ineffective policies that are destructive to his firm or organization rather than to admit his poor judgment in initiating them in the first place. A minister may resent criticisms from members of his congregation, the result being strained relationships and the erection of barriers.

In his biography of Florence Nightingale, Cecil Woodham-Smith relates how her efforts to improve the atrocious hospital conditions in the Crimea were hindered by official pride. In one of her letters home she wrote, "The real hardship of this place is that we have to do with men who are neither gentlemen nor men of education nor even men of business, nor men of feeling, whose only object is to keep themselves out of blame." One such man was a Dr. John Hall, who had submitted an official report stating that the condition of the hospitals was quite satisfactory. Once he had thus committed himself, he found himself forced to stand by his report; and with resentment he resisted every effort at reform that Miss Nightingale attempted to introduce.

How pride compels us to justify ourselves is also illustrated in a psychiatrist's comment concerning some physicians' attitudes towards deathbed scenes. He says, "At death scenes, doctors and nurses are frightened of families. They feel accused by the relatives because they are revealed as not being all-powerful. Doctors tend to keep families away to protect their own self-esteem."

This attitude of defensiveness, pride as self-justification, is the greatest obstacle to the two things needed most by fallen man. First, it prevents reconciliation to God, because it will not allow a man to repent. A man must be completely devoid of pride to acknowledge before his family and his friends and the entire community that the whole course of his life has been wrong, and that he is now entirely dependent upon and subject to a higher authority and power. Second, it is an obstacle to reconciliation between men, because it will not let the offender admit that he was wrong; it will not permit him to apologize and to ask forgiveness.

III. Self-Righteousness

The same pride that causes us to try to hide our sins and errors from others may eventually blind our own eyes to our faults and lead to an attitude of self-righteousness. We may come to have such a high opinion of ourselves that we feel we can do no wrong, that we have no sin. We say with the Pharisee, "God, I thank you that I am not a sinner like other men are" (Luke 18:11, paraphrase).

This is the reason that someone has called pride the sin of the virtuous person. Or as Luther put it, pride is the temptation of the white devil, who tempts us to keep the law and then to glory in it.

When the feeling of self-righteousness blinds us to our sins, it consequently makes us blind to grace. Herein lies the most serious result of the sin of pride. The pride of self-righteousness causes one to think that he merits or deserves salvation; therefore he cannot understand nor receive grace, which by its very nature can be recognized and received only by the unworthy and unrighteous. Thus the attitude of pride is the direct antithesis of the gospel of grace.

IV. Overcoming Pride

As the wise man says, the proud heart is sin. It is sin in all its forms: self-importance, self-justification, and self-righteousness. Each Christian must examine his life for the symptoms of the demon pride as discussed here, and do his utmost to eradicate it from his life. Truly "it is better to be of a humble spirit with the lowly, than to divide the spoil with the proud"; for "the reward of humility and the fear of the Lord are riches, honor and life" (Proverbs 16:19; 22:4).

The sin of pride can be overcome only when we surrender our proud hearts to the Holy Spirit and allow Him to remold them into meek and lowly hearts. How can we do this?

First, we must be agonizingly honest with ourselves. Pride is based on self-deception; it deceives us into thinking we are what we are not. The Lord said to tiny Edom, "Behold, I will make you small among the nations; you are greatly despised. The arrogance of your heart has deceived you, you who live in the clefts of the rock, in the loftiness of your dwelling place, who say in your heart, 'Who will bring me down to earth?' 'Though you build high like the eagle, though you set your nest among the stars, from there I will bring you down,' declares the Lord" (Obadiah 2-4). Jesus said, "And whoever exalts himself shall be humbled" (Matthew 23:12); i.e., his real worth shall be made manifest.

The exhortation of Paul and the example of Christ should help us to guard against pride, for Paul says, "For . . . I say to every man among you not to think more highly of himself than he ought to think" (Romans 12:3). Jesus the eternal Word and Lord of all could humble himself to the role of servant and wash His disciples' feet (John 13:2-15), probably at the very time they were arguing among themselves as to who was to be the greatest (Luke 22:24-27). Surely this is the scene Peter was recalling in his mind as he wrote, "All of you, clothe yourselves with humility toward one another, for God is opposed to the proud, but gives grace to the humble" (1 Peter 5:5).

The second thing we must do to overcome pride is to stop thinking about ourselves and about how we compare with others and about what other people think of us. Instead we must begin to take a sincere, unselfish interest in the needs and concerns of others. As Paul says, "Do nothing from selfishness or empty conceit, but with humility of mind let each of you regard one another as more important than himself; do not merely look out for your own personal interests, but also for the interests of others" (Philippians 2:3, 4).

Finally, instead of comparing ourselves with others, let us begin to compare ourselves with the true standard, Jesus Christ. Our puny self-importance and self-righteousness are obliterated by "the white, scorching purity of Christ." Charles Lamb is said to have remarked,

"If Shakespeare were to come into this room we should rise to our feet; if Christ were to enter we should fall upon our knees."

"And when I saw Him, I fell at His feet as a dead man" (Revelation 1:17).

> When I survey the wondrous cross
>   On which the Prince of glory died,
> My richest gain I count but loss,
>   And pour contempt on all my pride.